HOMELAND SECURITY
OPERATIONAL ANALYSIS CENTER

T0302895

A Review of Public Data About Terrorism and Targeted Violence to Meet U.S. Department of Homeland Security Mission Needs

JOE EYERMAN, RICHARD H. DONOHUE, NATHAN CHANDLER, TUCKER REESE

PREPARED FOR THE SCIENCE AND TECHNOLOGY DIRECTORATE, OFFICE OF SCIENCE AND ENGINEERING
APPROVED FOR PUBLIC RELEASE; DISTRIBUTION UNLIMITED

This research was published in 2021.

Preface

In September 2019, the U.S. Department of Homeland Security (DHS) released its *Strategic Framework for Countering Terrorism and Targeted Violence* (DHS, 2019c). The framework is the first national-level strategy to explicitly state that terrorism and targeted violence overlap, intersect, and interact as problems and require a shared set of solutions. The four goals of the framework are enumerated as follows:

- Goal 1: Understand the evolving terrorism and targeted violence threat environment, and support partners in the homeland security enterprise through this specialized knowledge.
- Goal 2: Prevent terrorists and other hostile actors from entering the United States, and deny them the opportunity to exploit the nation's trade, immigration, and domestic and international travel systems.
- Goal 3: Prevent terrorism and targeted violence.
- Goal 4: Enhance U.S. infrastructure protections and community preparedness. (DHS, 2019c, p. 2)

These goals require DHS to have access to data that can be used to better understand terrorism and targeted violence.

This report provides a review of DHS needs for data on terrorism and targeted violence, a review of existing prominent publicly available databases, and an assessment of gaps between DHS needs and the data in those databases. The objective of the review was to highlight broad gaps in the available data so that new programmatic and research needs could be identified to help address rapidly evolving threats. This report provides recommendations for improvements to sources of data to develop new databases and improve existing databases to support goals 1 (understand the evolving threat environment for terrorism and targeted violence) and 3 (prevent terrorism and targeted violence) of the DHS *Strategic Framework for Countering Terrorism and Targeted Violence*.

This research was sponsored by the U.S. Department of Homeland Security, Science and Technology Directorate, Office of Science and Engineering, and conducted within the Strategy, Policy, and Operations Program of the Homeland Security Operational Analysis Center (HSOAC) federally funded research and development center (FFRDC).

About the Homeland Security Operational Analysis Center

The Homeland Security Act of 2002 (Section 305 of Public Law 107-296, as codified at 6 U.S.C. § 185) authorizes the Secretary of Homeland Security, acting through the Under Secretary for Science and Technology, to establish one or more FFRDCs to provide independent analysis of homeland security issues. The RAND Corporation operates HSOAC as an FFRDC for DHS under contract HSHQDC-16-D-00007.

The HSOAC FFRDC provides the government with independent and objective analyses and advice in core areas important to the department in support of policy development, decisionmaking, alternative approaches, and new ideas on issues of significance. The HSOAC FFRDC also works with and supports other federal, state, local, tribal, and public- and private-sector organizations that make up the homeland security enterprise. The HSOAC FFRDC's research is undertaken by mutual consent with DHS and is organized as a set of discrete tasks. This report presents the results of research and analysis conducted under task order 70RSAT21FR0000003, "Independent Review of the Terrorism and Extremist Violence in the United States Data Needs."

The results presented in this report do not necessarily reflect official DHS opinion or policy. For more information on HSOAC, see www.rand.org/hsoac. For more information on this report, see www.rand.org/t/RRA1203-1.

Contents

Figures and Tables

Figures

Tables

Summary

The Homeland Security Operational Analysis Center (HSOAC) was asked by the U.S. Department of Homeland Security (DHS) Science and Technology Directorate to provide an independent review of DHS needs for data on terrorism and targeted violence,[1] including a review of existing prominent databases to identify gaps in data sources. The objective of the review was to quickly highlight broad gaps in the available data so that new programmatic and research needs could be identified to help address rapidly evolving threats. DHS and its individual components and offices have wide-ranging mission sets and operational environments. Accordingly, to protect the United States from the spectrum of threats of terrorism and targeted violence, there are very broad data needs to support efforts that include policy and prevention efforts, as well as actionable intelligence.

This report outlines the current state of those data sources on terrorism and targeted violence, describes DHS's data needs, and identifies gaps in existing data sources to support the DHS mission.

Approach

The HSOAC team used a three-part rapid assessment process to ascertain DHS's data needs, identify publicly available databases, assess the databases, and compare the databases with DHS needs. First, the HSOAC team reviewed the DHS *Strategic Framework for Countering Terrorism and Targeted Violence* (hereafter, the *DHS strategic framework*) and examined other strategic planning documents to understand the breadth of DHS data needs. This review included legislation that identified data needs related to terrorism and targeted violence. We also reviewed other pertinent DHS and HSOAC documents to further understand the data needs of the department. In a second and overlapping effort, we also reviewed published research and other public sources to identify publicly available unclassified databases that could inform the goals of the DHS strategic framework. This effort included a review of the quality-control techniques reported in the documentation for the databases. Third, we compared the publicly available data with DHS needs, identified gaps, and made recommendations for improvements to sources of data, integration of data, and standardization of data.

---

[1] *Strategic Framework for Countering Terrorism and Targeted Violence* defines *targeted violence* as "any incident of violence that implicates homeland security and/or [DHS] activities, and in which a known or knowable attacker selects a particular target prior to the violent attack" (DHS, 2019c, p. 4).

Research Design Attributes

This report was generated at the specific request of DHS to assist with the identification of inconsistencies between the data requirements in the DHS strategic framework and the publicly available unclassified databases on terrorism and targeted violence. To satisfy this request, we selected a rapid initial assessment process that would enable us to produce a report in approximately 90 days while still implementing a rigorous and systematic design.

The rapid initial assessment process required several design attributes to limit the scope of the project and allow us to meet this aggressive schedule:

- We focused primarily on the DHS strategic framework to identify DHS database needs, augmented with supplementary strategic and related documents.
- We conducted only very limited engagement with the creators and consumers of the publicly available databases.
- We used a systematic process to identify the databases that might meet DHS needs, but we limited our review to readily available, unclassified, published databases through searches of websites and the published literature.
- We selected a small subset (10) of the most-prominent publicly available databases and conducted a review of their self-reported quality control measures, using only their published methodological materials.
- We limited our recommendations to only those gaps that we could identify with this rapid process, noting as appropriate opportunities for future research that could improve the alignment of publicly available databases with DHS needs.

The rapid initial assessment process was designed to provide the required information on the abbreviated DHS schedule. However, these design attributes should be reexamined over time to determine whether they resulted in the exclusion of key information about the policy needs, gaps, or the available data. These design decisions reduced the scope to a feasible time frame but also limited the completeness of our review. A more complete set of DHS data needs could be identified through an expanded document review and engagement with a wider variety of data users throughout DHS and in other research organizations. A more complete understanding of the available data could be generated through a review of classified and commercial databases, in addition to the publicly available unclassified database reviewed here. Finally, a more detailed quality assessment could be conducted by reviewing more databases and through a more complete analysis of the different components of quality beyond our simple assessment of self-reported quality-control measures. We believe that these additional activities would extend the value of this report and are included in our recommendations for future research.

Findings

The DHS strategic framework provided us with a foundation for identifying needs for data on terrorism and targeted violence. Informed by the DHS strategic framework, we identified five prominent domains of interest that group threat types and allow closer examination of data sets to support DHS's needs:

- transnational terrorism
- extremist violence in the United States
- targeted violence
- cyberthreats for strategic or political purposes
- school shootings.

We mapped these domains across the needs of individual components (e.g., U.S. Customs and Border Protection, U.S. Immigration and Customs Enforcement) and to legislation, policy documents, and research reports.

The missions of the components and operating environments create the need for a broad understanding, supported by data, of the threats that face the United States. Data requirements might be codified in law or expressed through strategic goals; either way, DHS has a strong need for data to support policy and create actionable operational intelligence. These data needs span the gamut of incident types, actors, motivations, and tactics, techniques, and procedures.

Our review of unclassified terrorism databases shows that many sources are available to support DHS needs. However, some areas, such as cyberthreats and emerging technologies, might require new database construction. Furthermore, although the overall quality of the prominent databases is generally high, the quality assurance and study documentation standards are inconsistently applied, suggesting a need for clearly promulgated requirements.

Recommendations

Our assessment of the gaps between DHS data needs and the readily available data in unclassified published databases indicates four opportunities for DHS to improve the evidence-based study of terrorism and targeted violence:

- First, fund continued updates and maintenance to the prominent databases, and take opportunities to support new data construction, where needed, and alignment with prominent databases on terrorism and targeted violence, where appropriate, to cover apparent data needs for emerging areas, such as cyberthreats or new technologies.
- Second, require any DHS-supported study to uniformly apply quality and transparency standards across the prominent databases. The current, nonuniform application of such standards indicates an opportunity for DHS to clarify its expectations and potentially lead the discipline toward better standards of data collection.
- Third, invest in new data collection methods and an expedited process for identifying new data needs, and identify funding efforts to address these needs. Meeting DHS analytic needs requires, in many cases, timely data and novel measures of program effectiveness for counterterrorism. DHS can improve data's timeliness and relevance to emerging issues and program evaluations through this combination of actions.

Future Research

This study was designed as a rapid initial assessment with very limited scope concerning databases in the public domain. Future studies could provide a more thorough assessment of the challenges of aligning data collection efforts to DHS needs. Future studies on DHS data needs should include each of the following:

- an extended review of more-relevant DHS documentation about strategic goals that could be used to better understand data needs
- expanded discussions with DHS and academic data users to better understand their data needs and any limitations they have found in the available data
- inclusion of classified and commercial databases in the review process to identify additional data sources that might align with DHS needs
- assessment of more-prominent databases beyond the 10 used for study
- an expanded quality review to capture other dimensions of quality beyond self-reported quality-control measures
- an examination of the data included in each database.

Acknowledgments

This work benefited from the input and assistance of many people. Our sponsor, David Alexander, senior science adviser in the U.S. Department of Homeland Security Science and Technology Directorate, made this project possible. We wish to thank our reviewers, Javed Ali, Bruce Hoffman, Seamus Hughes, and Heather J. Williams, as well as Henry H. Willis, Brian Michael Jenkins, Victoria Greenfield, and Terrence Kelly, for their feedback throughout this work. Elizabeth May, Erica Robles, and Lisa Bernard provided considerable assistance with overall production management and with editing and formatting this report. Finally, we wish to thank Yousuf Abdelfatah and Ian Mitch for their contributions to the report.

Abbreviations

CBP	U.S. Customs and Border Protection
CBRN	chemical, biological, radiological, and nuclear
CISA	Cybersecurity and Infrastructure Security Agency
CTC	Combating Terrorism Center
CVE	countering violent extremism
DHS	U.S. Department of Homeland Security
ECDB	Extremist Crime Database
FBI	Federal Bureau of Investigation
FEMA	Federal Emergency Management Agency
FTO	foreign terrorist organization
FY	fiscal year
GED	Georeferenced Event Dataset
GTD	Global Terrorism Database
GW	George Washington University
HSOAC	Homeland Security Operational Analysis Center
HVE	homegrown violent extremist
I&A	Intelligence and Analysis
ICPSR	Inter-university Consortium for Political and Social Research
IPT	Investigative Project on Terrorism
LE	law enforcement
NCTC	National Counterterrorism Center
NDAA	National Defense Authorization Act
NGO	nongovernment organization

NTAC   National Threat Assessment Center

PTS   Political Terror Scale

QHSR   Quadrennial Homeland Security Review

SLTT   state, local, tribal, and territorial

START   National Consortium for the Study of Terrorism and Responses to Terrorism

TCO   transnational criminal organization

TSA   Transportation Security Administration

TTP   tactics, techniques, and procedures

UCDP   Uppsala Conflict Data Program

UCR   Uniform Crime Reporting

WMD   weapons of mass destruction

CHAPTER ONE

Introduction

As a result of increasing threats of terrorism and violent extremism, the U.S. Department of Homeland Security (DHS) adopted *Strategic Framework for Countering Terrorism and Targeted Violence* (DHS, 2019c) and public action plan (DHS, 2020a). Goals of the DHS strategic framework are as follows:

- Goal 1: Understand the evolving terrorism and targeted violence threat environment, and support partners in the homeland security enterprise through this specialized knowledge.
- Goal 2: Prevent terrorists and other hostile actors from entering the United States, and deny them the opportunity to exploit the nation's trade, immigration, and domestic and international travel systems.
- Goal 3: Prevent terrorism and targeted violence.
- Goal 4: Enhance U.S. infrastructure protections and community preparedness. (DHS, 2019c, p. 2)

These goals require DHS to utilize data that align with its strategic needs to understand the threat of terrorism and targeted violence. The Homeland Security Operational Analysis Center (HSOAC) was asked to provide support to DHS to analyze the prominent databases on terrorism and targeted violence and compare them with the needs of DHS users. The objective of the review was to quickly highlight broad gaps in the available data so that new programmatic and research needs could be identified to help address rapidly evolving threats.

HSOAC researchers completed an independent review of DHS needs for unclassified data to characterize and assess the threats to the United States from terrorism and targeted violence, a review of existing prominent databases, and an assessment of the alignment of existing publicly available data sets with data needs to identify any gaps in existing data availability from public sources and biases that might result. This report provides recommendations for improvements to sources of data to develop new databases and improve existing databases to support goals 1 (understand the evolving threat environment for terrorism and targeted violence) and 3 (prevent terrorism and targeted violence) in the DHS strategic framework.

Objectives

The objective was to quickly highlight broad gaps in the available data so that new program-matic and research needs could be identified to help address rapidly evolving threats. The research team fulfilled this objective by

- documenting DHS data needs, both mandated and implied
- identifying publicly available data sources on terrorism and targeted violence
- assessing prominent data sources to support DHS's needs.

In the process of completing these tasks, we were able to help DHS identify the gaps in current, publicly available data sources. This study was guided by the following research ques-tions, as applied to the databases in the public domain:

- What are the prominent data sources on terrorism and targeted violence?
- How do the prominent data sources align with DHS's current needs for understanding threats from terrorism and targeted violence?

The DHS Strategic Framework

In September 2019, DHS released its *Strategic Framework for Countering Terrorism and Tar-geted Violence* (DHS, 2019c). The framework is the first national-level strategy to explicitly state that terrorism and targeted violence overlap, intersect, and interact as problems and thus require a shared set of solutions. As specified in the DHS strategic framework, DHS will provide annual assessments to the relevant congressional committees; demonstrate measured improvements in its ability to understand current threats and accurately forecast emerging ones; detect threats before they reach the United States and deny terrorists' attempts to enter the United States; prevent terrorism and targeted violence in U.S. communities; and enhance U.S. infrastructure and community preparedness.

These goals require DHS to utilize data that align with its strategic needs to understand the threat of terrorism and targeted violence. Although many data sets exist, differences in the types of events included, time periods covered, the manner in which events are coded affect the data's relevance for DHS needs. These differences can also lead to gaps or perceived bias in available data; thus, opportunities exist in which trusted, open-source (i.e., publicly available) information could improve threat awareness and prevention efforts (Qureshi, 2020; Jackson et al., 2019; Hull, 2020). As a result, DHS seeks improved sources of publicly available data to support the goals of the DHS strategic framework.

Research Overview

The HSOAC team used a three-part rapid assessment process to ascertain DHS's data needs, identify publicly available databases, assess the databases, and compare the databases with DHS needs. First, the HSOAC team reviewed the DHS *Strategic Framework for Countering Terrorism and Targeted Violence* (hereafter, the *DHS strategic framework*) and examined other strategic planning documents to understand the breadth of DHS data needs. This review included legislation that identified data needs related to terrorism and targeted violence. We also reviewed other pertinent DHS and HSOAC documents to further understand the data needs of the department. In a second and overlapping effort, we also reviewed published research and other public sources to identify publicly available unclassified databases that could inform the goals of the DHS strategic framework. This effort included a review of the quality-control techniques reported in the documentation for the databases. Third, we compared the publicly available data with DHS needs, identified gaps, and made recommendations for improvements to sources of data, integration of data, and standardization of data.

Organization of This Report

This report documents the process we used to meet the project objectives and presents our findings and recommendations from that process. In Chapter Two, we assess the DHS data needs as expressed in the DHS strategic framework and related strategic documents. In Chapter Three, we review the current state of databases on terrorism and targeted violence and provide an assessment of the data quality of the most-prominent databases. In Chapter Four, we compare DHS needs with the available data to identify gaps and map a plan to guide future data collection efforts to better align with DHS requirements.

CHAPTER TWO

A Review of Department of Homeland Security Data Needs

In our efforts to define DHS data needs, we commenced by conducting a targeted review of DHS policy and planning documents. The review was guided by the DHS strategic framework. To gain an understanding of data needs across DHS operational and support components, we examined 15 DHS strategic planning documents. We then reviewed legislation from fiscal years (FYs) 2015 through 2020 that mandates or suggests data needs pertinent to DHS as they relate to terrorism or targeted violence. Lastly, we included other pertinent DHS and HSOAC documents to further understand the data needs of the department.

Strategic Framework for Countering Terrorism and Targeted Violence

The DHS strategic framework sets forth four goals:

- Goal 1: Understand the evolving terrorism and targeted violence threat environment, and support partners in the homeland security enterprise through this specialized knowledge.
- Goal 2: Prevent terrorists and other hostile actors from entering the United States, and deny them the opportunity to exploit the Nation's trade, immigration, and domestic and international travel systems.
- Goal 3: Prevent terrorism and targeted violence.
- Goal 4: Enhance U.S. infrastructure protections and community preparedness. (DHS, 2019c, p. 2)

Although the DHS strategic framework does not specify exact variables of interest, it does offer guidance as to what types of data are likely helpful in achieving these four goals. We reviewed the DHS strategic framework for specific language pertaining to the data needs of DHS. Our review uncovered four core categories of data needs:

- actors (i.e., who poses a threat to the United States?)
- targets (i.e., what are the targets of interest?)
- tactics, techniques, and procedures (TTPs) (i.e., how are attacks carried out?)
- motivation (i.e., what are the reasons for terrorism and targeted violence?).

Table 2.1 further describes these categories.

The DHS strategic framework does not specifically name all types of actors, targets, TTPs, or motivations. Accordingly, Table 2.1 includes only language specific to the DHS stra-

Table 2.1
Categories of Data Needs Captured in *Strategic Framework for Countering Terrorism and Targeted Violence*

Core Category	Example of Data Needed
Actors (actual and potential) (type and characteristics)	• FTOs • HVEs • Radical Islamists • White supremacists • Watch-listed individuals • Insider threats • Lone attackers • Terrorist travel • Motivation • Mental health background • Life stressors • Communications/leakage • Recidivism
Targets (actual and potential)	• Communities • Schools • Places of worship • Public gatherings • Special events • Critical infrastructure • Transportation systems • Maritime domain
TTPs	• Technologies used for attacks • Use of unmanned systems • WMD attacks • CBRN threat • Firearms • Interfering with mass transit, supply chain networks, and critical infrastructure
Motivation	• Race • Ethnicity • Antigovernment or anti-authority • Religion • Personal grievances • No clear motive • Other ideologies

SOURCE: Authors' analysis of the DHS strategic framework (DHS, 2019c).

NOTE: FTO = foreign terrorist organization. HVE = homegrown violent extremist. WMD = weapons of mass destruction. CBRN = chemical, biological, radiological, and nuclear. The terms HVE and domestic violent extremist (discussed later) were defined in the October 2020 *Homeland Threat Assessment*:

> Domestic Violent Extremist (DVE): An individual based and operating primarily within the United States or its territories without direction or inspiration from a foreign terrorist group or other foreign power who seeks to further political or social goals wholly or in part through unlawful acts of force or violence. The mere advocacy of political or social positions, political activism, use of strong rhetoric, or generalized philosophic embrace of violent tactics may not constitute extremism, and may be constitutionally protected.

> Homegrown Violent Extremist (HVE): A person of any citizenship who has lived and/or operated primarily in the United States or its territories who advocates, is engaged in, or is preparing to engage in ideologically-motivated terrorist activities (including providing support to terrorism) in furtherance of political or social objectives promoted by a foreign terrorist organization (FTO), but is acting independently of direction by an FTO. HVEs are distinct from traditional domestic terrorists who engage in unlawful acts of violence to intimidate civilian populations or attempt to influence domestic policy without direction from or influence from a foreign actor. (DHS, 2020b, p. 17)

tegic framework (e.g., signaling a need for an understanding of "radical Islamists" or "white supremacists").[1] At the same time, the inclusion of attacks that lack a motive or are motivated by "other ideologies" widens the data needs for DHS, today and in the future, to support the department's ability to protect the country.

We divided the data needs of DHS, based on the DHS strategic framework, into five domains:

- transnational terrorism: We define *transnational terrorism* as terrorist activities that are initiated in another country but directly affect the United States. According to Rosendorff and Sandler, "Through its perpetrators, victims, or audience, transnational terrorism has implications for two or more countries. If an incident starts in one country but terminates in another (e.g., 9/11 and 3/11), then the incident is a transnational terrorist event" (Rosendorff and Sandler, 2005, p. 172; see also Enders, Sandler, and Gaibulloev, 2011).

- extremist violence in the United States: The Federal Bureau of Investigation (FBI) has described extremist violence as "encouraging, condoning, justifying, or supporting the commission of a violent act to achieve political, ideological, religious, social, or economic goals" (FBI, undated). This domain includes domestic violent extremists and HVEs and, as noted in the FBI's November 2020 National Defense Authorization Act (NDAA) report on domestic terrorism,
  - racially or ethnically motivated violent extremism
  - antigovernment or anti-authority violent extremism
  - animal rights–related or environmental violent extremism
  - abortion-related violent extremism
  - all other domestic terrorism threats.

- targeted violence: As of the writing of this report, DHS defines *targeted violence*, in "Strategic Framework for Countering Terrorism and Targeted Violence: Public Action Plan," as follows: "The Department generally uses the term to refer to any incident of violence that implicates homeland security and/or DHS activities in which a known or knowable attacker selects a particular target prior to the violent attack" (DHS, 2020a, p. i). The DHS strategic framework includes "attacks on schools, house of worship, public spaces, and transportation systems, and other forms of racially, ethnically, and religiously motivated violence that can overlap and intersect with terrorism" in its description of targeted violence (DHS, 2019c, p. 1) and states the following:

  > For purposes of this Strategy, targeted violence refers to any incident of violence that implicates homeland security and/or U.S. Department of Homeland Security (DHS) activities, and in which a known or knowable attacker selects a particular target prior to the violent attack. Unlike terrorism, targeted violence includes attacks otherwise lacking a clearly discernible political, ideological, or religious motivation, but that are of such severity and magnitude as to suggest an intent to inflict a degree of mass injury, destruction, or death commensurate with known terrorist tactics. (DHS, 2019c, p. 4)

---

[1]   These terms are directly outlined in the DHS strategic framework. Titles, terms, and definitions might change in the future. However, we recognize that there is specific language in the DHS strategic framework that encompasses a breadth of current and future motivations for terrorism and targeted violence.

- cyberthreats for strategic or political purposes: This threat relates to malicious activities that affect the cyber domain. The October 2020 *Homeland Threat Assessment* (DHS, 2020b) refers to an "array of cyber-enabled threats designed to access sensitive information, steal money, and force ransom payments" (p. 8).
- school shootings: We separated shootings that occur in school settings from targeted violence because of the public fear they cause, the growth in attention around these incidents since the 1990s, and DHS's focus on these events through National Threat Assessment Center (NTAC) initiatives.

Identifying the most-prominent data sources across areas of terrorism and targeted violence allows us to provide a cross-threat analysis of (1) quality of and (2) gaps in the data. Our methodology for refining and down-selecting data sources for additional analysis based on these domains is described in detail in Chapter Three. We supplemented our analysis of the DHS strategic framework by also examining its public action plan. The plan outlines specific data needs to meet the four goals set forth in the DHS strategic framework. In Table 2.2, we map the tasks from the action plan to strategic goals of DHS, the five domains we identified, and conceptual data needs to support the tasks. It should be noted that the tasks and associated data needs, mapped by domain, underscore the complexities that DHS faces in carrying out the DHS strategic framework and protecting the United States. The tasks vary from public-facing threat assessments to supporting societal resistance to violent extremism, a fact that further demonstrates the wide spectrum of actions DHS must lead and the data to support such efforts.

DHS Mission and Goals

We reviewed documents pertinent to DHS's mission and goals to provide context for the department's overall data needs. DHS's guiding principles, especially the first two (excerpted here), highlight the broad mission sets and critical nature of the work the department undertakes to prepare and respond to threats:

> Champion "Relentless Resilience" for All Threats and Hazards: DHS will remain resolute against today's threats and hazards by keeping pace with our adversaries and preparing for those of tomorrow by identifying and confronting systemic risk, ensuring the Nation's citizens remain resilient, building redundancy and resilience into community lifelines, and raising the baseline of our security across the board—and across the world.

> Reduce the Nation's Risk to Homeland Security Dangers: DHS will mitigate risks to the Homeland by interdicting threats, hardening assets to eliminate vulnerabilities, and enhancing rapid recovery efforts to reduce potential consequences from physical attacks, natural disasters, and cyber incidents. (DHS, 2019a)

From this guidance alone, it is clear that it will be necessary to identify historical threats that might reoccur (whether using the same TTPs or following the same ideology), current threats, and risks of terrorism and targeted violence on the horizon. To understand the data

Table 2.2
Data Needs for the Public Action Plan

Goal	Task	Domain					Data Need
		Transnational Terrorism	Extremist Violence in the United States	Targeted Violence	Cyberthreats for Strategic or Political Purposes	School Shootings	
Understand the evolving terrorism and targeted violence threat environment, and support partners in the homeland security enterprise through specialized knowledge.	Develop an annual state of Homeland Threat Assessment.	x	x	x	x	x	Valid, reliable data from multiple sources covering a variety of crimes and threats
	Craft a new definition of targeted violence.			x		x	Lessons learned from previous incidents, including target hardening and immediate response
	Enhance DHS methods of collecting and analyzing data and information on relevant patterns of violence.	x	x	x	x	x	Valid, reliable data from multiple sources covering a variety of crimes and threats
Prevent terrorists and other hostile actors from entering the United States, and deny them the opportunity to exploit the U.S. trade, immigration, and domestic and international travel systems.	Reach beyond U.S. borders and prioritize interoperability of information sharing.[a]	x					International/transnational threat data
	Improve vetting and screening capabilities.[a]	x					Intelligence-based products
	Prevent insider threats.[a]				x		

Table 2.2—Continued

Goal	Task	Domain					Data Need
		Transnational Terrorism	Extremist Violence in the United States	Targeted Violence	Cyberthreats for Strategic or Political Purposes	School Shootings	
Prevent terrorism and targeted violence.	Strengthen societal resistance to the drivers of violent extremism and ensure broad awareness of the threat of terrorism and targeted violence. Form partnerships that support locally based prevention efforts.	X	X	X		X	Historical and current data on impetus for terrorism and violent extremism; information on current threats; information on prevention programs and their effectiveness
	Increase societal awareness of violent extremism and mobilization to violence.	X	X	X		X	Knowledge of the threat environment, including risk factors and behavioral indicators
	Support countermessaging efforts by technology companies, NGOs, and civic partners.	X	X	X	X	X	Information on effective messaging for terrorism and targeted violence based on historical data
	Enhance grant program support with SLTT LE, and emergency management partners.	X	X	X		X	Effectiveness and evaluations of grant programs
	Develop a media and information literacy toolkit and bolster information sharing about foreign disinformation campaigns.	X	X	X			Information on foreign adversaries' use of various forms of media to stoke tension, unrest, or violence

Table 2.2—Continued

Goal	Task	Domain					Data Need
		Transnational Terrorism	Extremist Violence in the United States	Targeted Violence	Cyberthreats for Strategic or Political Purposes	School Shootings	
Enhance U.S. infrastructure protections and community preparedness.	Enable preparedness.	x	x	x	x	x	Information across the threat and hazard spectrum; lessons learned from previous incidents, including target hardening and immediate response.
	Enhance security of soft targets.	x	x	x		x	Information on past attacks on soft target types, including TTPs
	Defend against threats from unmanned systems and other emerging technologies.	x	x	x	x		Information on current systems, threats, and attacks related to unmanned systems

NOTE: NGO = nongovernmental organization. SLTT = state, local, tribal, and territorial. LE = law enforcement.
[a] Primarily an intelligence or LE-sensitive data-based task.

needs of the department in the present and near future specifically, we reviewed DHS's *Strategic Plan: Fiscal Years 2020–2024*, which outlines six primary strategic goals:

- Counter terrorism and homeland security threats.
- Secure U.S. borders and approaches.
- Secure cyberspace and critical infrastructure.
- Preserve and uphold the nation's prosperity and economic security.
- Strengthen preparedness and resilience.
- Champion the DHS workforce and strengthen the department (DHS, 2019b, p. 7).

Of these, the first five directly relate to the need for data to help understand terrorist threats and targeted violence. The sixth also highlights the importance of strong data sets to support the department. The overall goals of DHS clearly align with the domains we have identified for analysis. For example, the need to counter terrorism and homeland security threats has a clear nexus to a need for information on transnational terrorism, extremist violence in the United States, targeted violence, and school shootings. DHS's third strategic goal highlights the need for information on cyberthreats for strategic or political purposes. We argue that there is a broad need for data to validate policy and security missions for DHS that address actors, threats, targets, and motivations.

Component Strategic Plans

We also reviewed strategic plans by components and, where available and current, individual agencies within DHS components to determine data needs. We focused primarily on the data needs for operational components for this analysis because they have varying areas of responsibility.

Specific data needs were described in detail in several of the component-specific strategic documents. Although none of them specifically mentions a new or existing database of terrorism or targeted violence, various data and data sets could further the missions of the components. Specifically, U.S. Customs and Border Protection (CBP) called for "better integrating and analyzing data across the interagency community to create a common operating picture that can be actioned at both the field and the headquarters level" (CBP, 2019, p. 8). Although this has a clear nexus to *intelligence*, it also speaks to the need for data to understand threats to CBP's mission, as well as to its partners—namely, other federal and SLTT LE agencies. Further, CBP outlined the need for increased data and analytics specific to the border and trade enforcement for broad, strategic needs (e.g., policy decisions), as well as tactical needs (e.g., intelligence). The Cybersecurity and Infrastructure Security Agency's (CISA's) mission to protect critical infrastructure also aligns with a clear need for data: As stated in CISA's strategic vision document, "our efforts must be data-driven, threat-informed, and validated by our stakeholders" (CISA, 2019, p. 5). Table 2.3 summarizes our findings.

Strategic and tactical data needs are also explicitly laid out in other strategic planning documents. Where data needs are not explicitly stated are clear areas in which data are supportive of component needs. For example, the TSA documents do not speak to terrorism or targeted violence databases directly, but they are likely to be informed by them.

We also reviewed strategic documents for select nonoperational components. We have included an analysis for the Countering Weapons of Mass Destruction Office, the Federal Law Enforcement Training Centers, and the Office of Intelligence and Analysis (I&A) in Table 2.4.

Table 2.3
Data Needs to Support Operational Components' Strategic Goals

Operational Component	Primary Area of Responsibility	Domain					Data Needs to Support Strategic Plan
		Transnational Terrorism	Extremist Violence in the United States	Targeted Violence	Cyberthreats for Strategic or Political Purposes	School Shootings	
CBP	• Border • Trade • Travel	X			X		• Combat illicit cross-border activity. • Address cyber and e-commerce threats. • Gather predictive and mission-supporting intelligence. • Collect actionable data and intelligence for CBP and interagency partners in the strategic and tactical realms.
CISA	• Cybersecurity • Critical infrastructure	X	X	X	X	X	• Support risk prioritization. • Understand threats. • Inform prevention, mitigation, and response efforts. • Support planning and preparedness for special events and mass gatherings.
FEMA	• All hazards[a]	X	X	X	X		• Understand local and community risks. • Consider the evolving threat environment, from low-tech dangers to complex incidents. • Share lessons learned from after-action reports.
ICE	• Border • Customs • Trade • Immigration	X	X	X	X		• Support investigative strategies focusing on national security and public safety threats. • Manage security risks: screening and vetting to identify those with ties to terrorism or criminal activities (in the United States and abroad). • Prevent immigration-related fraud. • Observe TCOs domestically and internationally. • Track cybercrime threats. • Support joint terrorism task forces and work with other federal and SLTT agencies.

Table 2.3—Continued

Operational Component	Primary Area of Responsibility	Domain					Data Needs to Support Strategic Plan
		Transnational Terrorism	Extremist Violence in the United States	Targeted Violence	Cyberthreats for Strategic or Political Purposes	School Shootings	
TSA[b]	• Transportation systems	x	x	x			• Drive operations through intelligence. • Improve effectiveness of security in conjunction with transportation stakeholders. • Inform measures, processes, and programs. • Enhance vetting capabilities. • Strengthen physical and cybersecurity measures. • Identify trends, gaps, and vulnerabilities of transportation systems.
U.S. Citizenship and Immigration Services	• The immigration system	x					• Identify vulnerabilities in the immigration system (integrity, vetting). • Conduct threat and fraud detection and monitoring. • Enhance information exchange.
U.S. Coast Guard	• Maritime	x			x		• Identify TCOs and other malicious nonstate actors in the maritime domain. • Identify state and nonstate threats (especially in the cyber domain). • Support situational awareness. • Optimize deployment planning. • Act on lessons learned and best practices from previous events.

Table 2.3—Continued

Operational Component	Primary Area of Responsibility	Domain						Data Needs to Support Strategic Plan
		Transnational Terrorism	Extremist Violence in the United States	Targeted Violence	Cyberthreats for Strategic or Political Purposes	School Shootings		
U.S. Secret Service	• Financial infrastructure • Personal protection for U.S. and world leaders	x	x	x	x	x		• Enhance situational awareness. • Keep abreast of the continuously changing threat environment. • Track adversary use of technology (three-dimensional printing of weapons, bioterrorism, low-cost surveillance techniques). • Prevent conventional attacks (e.g., vehicle rammings, cyberintrusion, explosive ordnance). • Support NTAC initiatives and reports. • Create a technology foresight and innovation program.

SOURCE: Authors' analysis of CBP, 2019; CISA, 2019; Federal Emergency Management Agency (FEMA), 2018; U.S. Immigration and Customs Enforcement (ICE), 2020; Transportation Security Administration (TSA), undated; TSA, 2020b; U.S. Citizenship and Immigration Services, undated; U.S. Coast Guard; undated; U.S. Secret Service, 2018.

NOTE: TCO = transnational criminal organization.

[a] FEMA is tasked with responding to natural hazards (e.g., disasters, such as hurricanes) and human-caused hazards (such as terrorism).

[b] TSA information is from *TSA Strategy 2018–2026* (TSA, undated) and *Administrator's Intent 2.0* (TSA, 2020b).

Table 2.4
Data Needs to Support Nonoperational Components' Strategic Goals

Nonoperational Component	Primary Area of Responsibility	Domain					Data Needs to Support Strategic Plan
		Transnational Terrorism	Extremist Violence in the United States	Targeted Violence	Cyberthreats for Strategic or Political Purposes	School Shootings	
Countering Weapons of Mass Destruction Office	• WMD threats • CBRN preparedness • Health security threats	x	x				• Mine data from a variety of databases related to the CBRN threat. • Inform policy on WMD and health security strategy. • Enhance subject-matter expertise to assist in crises.
Federal Law Enforcement Training Centers	• Training DHS LEOs • Training other federal LEOs • Training SLTT LEOs	x	x	x	x	x	• Inform training management decisions.
I&A	• Intelligence	x	x	x	x	x	• Support anticipatory, strategic, and operational intelligence across I&A's topical mission areas.

SOURCES: Authors' analysis of Countering Weapons of Mass Destruction Office, undated; Federal Law Enforcement Training Centers, undated; I&A, 2020.

NOTE: LEO = LE officer.

Legislation

We reviewed recent laws of interest from the past three sessions of Congress, spanning from 2015 to 2020. During this time, four laws of interest were passed related to terrorism, as well as language regarding terrorism found in nine appropriation bills. The laws require or dictate certain data, while the appropriation bills explain congressional intent. We supplemented this by conducting a keyword search for topics related to terrorism and targeted violence in the NDAAs for the same time frame.

Laws

We identified four laws that link DHS to terrorism or targeted violence and are mapped to our domains in Table 2.5. Three of the four laws that we reviewed speak directly to DHS's data needs: the Vehicular Terrorism Prevention Act of 2018 (Pub. L. 115-400), the DHS Data Framework Act of 2018 (Pub. L. 115-331), and the Northern Border Security Review Act (Pub. L. 114-267, 2016).[2] The first act speaks to TTPs—in this case, the use of a vehicle during a terrorist act. The data needs dictated by this act relate to a strategy that DHS required to

Table 2.5
Laws of Interest, 2015–2020

Law Name	Domain					Data Need
	Transnational Terrorism	Extremist Violence in the United States	Targeted Violence	Cyberthreats for Strategic or Political Purposes	School Shootings	
DHS Field Engagement Accountability Act of 2020	x	x	x			Not applicable; law denotes personnel support
Vehicular Terrorism Prevention Act of 2018	x	x	x			Examination of current threats from vehicular terrorism; information sharing with interagency and private-sector partners
DHS Data Framework Act of 2018						Applicable to integration of data sets and systems
Northern Border Security Review Act	x		x			Data on actors and groups, the related threat environment, and shared information with community and SLTT stakeholders

---

[2]   The fourth law, the DHS Field Engagement Accountability Act (Pub. L. 116-116, 2020), focuses primarily on personnel support and is not directly relevant to the scope of this study.

combat this threat. The strategy itself was mandated to include (1) an examination of the threat, (2) methods to improve DHS's information sharing with partners about this threat, and (3) training that can be provided by DHS to respond to vehicular terrorism.

These laws relate directly to domains of interest we have identified. They also map to particular areas we identified in Table 2.1 that originated in the DHS strategic framework. Vehicular terrorism, for example, falls under TTPs, while the Northern Border Security Review Act relates to actors and, broadly, targets.

Appropriation Bills

Following the review of laws that were passed during the past three sessions of Congress, we reviewed appropriation report language from the past five years.

The FY 2021 Senate bill clearly outlines where data are needed to support briefings for the Office for Targeted Violence and Terrorism Prevention, with a focus on "domestic terrorism." The language in the bill reflects some changing priorities based on current or perceived threats, including a focus on extremist infiltration of LE organizations. The FY 2020 Senate bill also includes language specific to preventing *all* forms of terrorism, both international and domestic, as well as targeted violence. Although this scope is broad, there is no specification for any type of data. Rather, the data needed to support these directives are implied.

The language in earlier bills might have been less specific, but there is still a need to support the directives with pertinent, validated data. Table 2.6 describes the specific and implied data needs from the appropriation bills we reviewed in Table 2.5.

Similar to the laws we discussed above, these bills also directly relate to the four core categories identified in the DHS strategic framework: (1) actors, such as through supporting countering violent extremism (CVE) programs; (2) targets, such as urban areas; (3) TTPs, including cyberattacks; and (4) motivation, such as racially driven acts.

National Defense Authorization Acts

We also conducted a search of keywords related to terrorism and targeted violence in NDAAs from the past five FYs. The search yielded three documents from FYs 2018 through 2020 that included language pertinent to DHS and terrorism and targeted violence. We summarize domains and data needs (implied and implicit) based on NDAAs from the past five years in Table 2.7.

There is a statutory basis for data needs from the FY 2020 NDAA. In particular, the NDAA calls for DHS and the FBI to conduct a strategic intelligence assessment of domestic terrorism. The NDAA requires a report from DHS and the FBI, which naturally requires data specific to the domestic terrorism threat. The FY 2020 NDAA, in fact, specifically requires analysis of "each completed or attempted incident of domestic terrorism that has occurred in the United States" since 2009:

> (I) a description of such incident; (II) the date and location of such incident; (III) the number and type of completed and attempted Federal nonviolent crimes committed during such incident; (IV) the number and type of completed and attempted Federal and State property crimes committed during such incident, including an estimate of economic damages resulting from such crimes; and (V) the number and type of completed and attempted Federal violent crimes committed during such incident, including the number of people injured or killed as a result of such crimes. (Pub. L. 116-116, 2020, § 5602[4][A][i])

Table 2.6
Appropriation Language

| | Domain | | | | | |
Bill	Transnational Terrorism	Extremist Violence in the United States	Targeted Violence	Cyberthreats for Strategic or Political Purposes	School Shootings	Data Need
FY 2021 Senate		x	x			Broad description of threats and sharing of threats with partners and the public; data to feed into training needs; interagency information sharing; analysis of completed and attempted incidents of domestic terrorism
FY 2020 Senate	x	x	x			Data on international and domestic terrorist threats; targeted violence, especially that which is racially motivated; the manner in which threats are communicated and used in training material
FY 2019 House	x					Number of terrorist acts prevented by cooperation of aliens
FY 2018 Senate	x			x		Data to measure national preparedness (specific to FEMA) with respect to terrorist attacks, cybersecurity, or other incidents
FY 2017 House	x	x	x			Data to support CVE efforts and for preparing for complex, coordinated terrorist attacks; data to support FEMA's efforts to conduct assessments of terrorist threats and vulnerabilities to urban areas
FY 2017 Senate	x	x	x	x		Incidents of unauthorized use of a security identification display area; details on the risk to spectator sports and significant effects; information on refugees and asylum seekers who have subsequent terrorist affiliations

Table 2.7
Language from National Defense Authorization Act

NDAA	Domain					Data Need
	Transnational Terrorism	Extremist Violence in the United States	Targeted Violence	Cyberthreats for Strategic or Political Purposes	School Shootings	
FY 2020	x	x	x			To develop methodologies to track domestic terrorism, including definitions; information to support intelligence and intelligence products related to terrorism; analysis of domestic terrorism from 2009 to the present (incidents and investigations)
FY 2018	x		x			To support interagency efforts to combat violent extremism
FY 2017	x					To understand the evolving terrorist threat, including terrorist and foreign-fighter travel to and from the United States

SOURCE: Authors' analysis of NDAAs (Pub. L. 116-92, 2019; Pub. L. 115-91, 2017; and Pub. L. 114-328, 2016).

and

(I) an identification of each assessment, preliminary investigation, full investigation, and enterprise investigation with a nexus to domestic terrorism opened, pending, or closed by the Federal Bureau of Investigation; (II) the number of assessments or investigations identified under subclause (I) associated with each domestic terrorism investigative classification (including subcategories); (III) the number of assessments or investigations described in subclause (II) initiated as a result of a referral or investigation by a Federal, State, local, Tribal, territorial, or foreign government, of a hate crime; (IV) the number of Federal criminal charges with a nexus to domestic terrorism, including the number of indictments and complaints associated with each domestic terrorism investigative classification (including subcategories), a summary of the allegations contained in each such indictment, the disposition of the prosecution, and, if applicable, the sentence imposed as a result of a conviction on such charges; (V) referrals of incidents of domestic terrorism by or to State, local, Tribal, territorial, or foreign governments, to or by departments or agencies of the Federal Government, for investigation or prosecution, including the number of such referrals associated with each domestic terrorism investigation classification (including any subcategories), and a summary of each such referral that includes the rationale for such referral and the disposition of the applicable Federal investigation or prosecution; (VI) intelligence products produced by the intelligence community relating to domestic terrorism, including, with respect to the Federal Bureau of Investigation, the number of such products associated with each domestic terrorism investigative classification (including any subcategories). (Pub. L. 116-116, 2020, § 5602[4][A][ii])

Other DHS or DHS-Related Publications

We evaluated other DHS and DHS-related publications to further understand the needs of the department. These include policy documents, threat assessments, and publicly available outside studies that detail data needs or requirements. Although they do not encompass every mission or document specific to terrorism and targeted violence, they capture many of DHS's multiple efforts to protect the country, and they convey the data needed to support these endeavors.

According to our examination of the threats that the United States faces as detailed in the Quadrennial Homeland Security Review (QHSR) (DHS, 2014), strategic priorities for DHS included the following (p. 16):

- An updated posture to address the increasingly decentralized terrorist threat;
- A strengthened path forward for cybersecurity that acknowledges the increasing interdependencies among critical systems and networks;
- A homeland security strategy to manage the urgent and growing risk of biological threats and hazards;
- A risk segmentation approach to securing and managing flows of people and goods into and out of the United States; and,
- A new framework for improving the efficiency and effectiveness of our mission execution through public-private partnerships.

The QHSR, like other documents, highlights both the enduring and evolving terrorist threats to the United States. This is reflected in a continued focus on groups or actors, such as al Qaeda, and TTPs that include the use of improvised explosive devices, as well as the risks to critical infrastructure from threats to cyberspace. The QHSR also aims to mature homeland security; one of the key areas identified is conducting research and development. This includes studying threats, developing solutions, and working with research partners.

Homeland Threat Assessment (DHS, 2020b) defines seven primary threats:

- cyber
- foreign-influence activity
- economic security
- terrorism
- TCOs
- illegal immigration
- natural disasters.

Some of these continue to reflect traditional threats to the United States, while emerging threats are also documented. For example, this document also describes threats from exploitation of constitutionally protected speech by violent extremists, as well as infectious diseases. Although not all threats to the United States are directly tied to terrorism or targeted violence (such as natural disasters and infectious diseases), the threats that the United States faces are both broad and varied.

Other documentation from DHS provides a more limited scope of particular threats. For example, NTAC research has focused on particular targets of interest, such as schools (Vossekuil et al., 2002; Pollack, Modzeleski, and Rooney, 2008; Drysdale, Modzeleski, and

Simons, 2010; Alathari, Drysdale, Blair, et al., 2018; Alathari, Drysdale, Driscoll, Blair, Carlock, et al., 2019), public spaces (Alathari, Blair, et al., 2018; Alathari, Driscoll, et al., 2019; Alathari, Drysdale, Driscoll, Blair, Mauldin, et al., 2020), and federal facilities (NTAC, 2015). The needs for data on threats to schools, public spaces, and federal facilities map not only to the five domains we have identified but also to the four core categories—actors, targets, TTPs, and motivations—that we identified in our analysis of the DHS strategic framework (see Table 2.1). A recent example of this can be found in an NTAC report on mass attacks in public spaces (Alathari, Drysdale, Driscoll, Blair, Mauldin, et al., 2020). To be able to produce such a report and understand the threat of this type, there is a need for comprehensive incident-level data: weapon used, location, timing, targeting, resolution, and motives. In addition, attacker-level data are required: demographics, employment history, substance use, criminal history, mental health, beliefs, online influence, life stressors, threats and leakage, social isolation, and behaviors that elicited concern. Analysis based on this type of data is helpful in providing community-level and LE response.

We also reviewed other relevant DHS documents to understand how data can support the mission sets. FEMA's *2020 National Preparedness Report* (DHS, 2020c) details specific areas of risk; data play a significant role in determining risk and prevention of hazards. Although many of the hazards are natural, human-caused hazards include active-shooter attacks and insider threats. DHS's *Northern Border Strategy* (DHS, 2018) focuses on a geographically large area of interest with the stated objective of improving "coordination, integration, and analysis across domestic and international domain surveillance and information-sharing system" (p. 11). The strategy also includes language specifying the use of open-source databases to fulfill the objective. The data needs are also specified across air, land, maritime, and cyber operating environments. This is detailed in TSA's *2020 Biennial National Strategy for Transportation Security* (TSA, 2020a), which takes a risk-based approach to aviation, maritime, surface, and intermodal threats. Although its focus is on quickly delivering actionable intelligence, the strategy references past terrorist attacks to inform risk. In planning for threats to these areas, such data as traditional risk scenarios (e.g., small-boat attacks) and emerging threats (e.g., unmanned aircraft systems and cyberattacks) will help to support DHS efforts.

The Five Country Research and Development Terrorism Prevention Meeting, in which DHS took part, included research agendas from all the participants. In particular, it highlighted the National Institute of Justice study efforts that have lent significant understanding (and corresponding data) for terrorism and targeted violence. However, there was still an outstanding need to conduct research independently and in collaboration with international partners.

DHS initiatives, such as the National Suspicious Activity Reporting Initiative, the Campus Resilience Program, and Counter–Improvised Explosive Device Training and Awareness efforts represent additional areas that would be—and are—supported by relevant data on terrorism and targeted violence. Again, these represent a sample of DHS functional areas, not the universe of programs, in which databases would be helpful to the department's needs.

Other HSOAC and RAND reports highlight data needs related to this mission of DHS. Specifically, *Practical Terrorism Prevention: Reexamining U.S. National Approaches to Addressing the Threat of Ideologically Motivated Violence* (Jackson et al., 2019) outlines data needs related to DHS and interagency partners in their CVE efforts. To accomplish these efforts, the nature of the threat must be identified. The authors did this by examining START's Profiles of Individual Radicalization in the United States database, New America's data collection efforts (Bergen, Ford, et al., 2020), U.S. government terrorist threat bulletins, START's Global Terrorism Database (GTD) (Miller, LaFree, and Dugan, undated), the George Washington University (GW) Extremism Tracker (GW Program on Extremism, 2021), and other sources. These data sources permitted an informed understanding of threats and thus the ability to examine terrorism prevention. The RAND report *Homeland Security National Risk Characterization* (Willis et al., 2018) also specifies data needs based on hazards and risk attributes that, when combined into the model shown in Figure 2.1, support a national risk characterization.

This risk characterization is broad enough to cover hazards but detailed enough that it can be applied to threats of terrorism and targeted violence. The issues we identify later in this report with respect to data and characterization are reflected in gaps in the process.

Conclusion

The DHS strategic framework identifies broad and evolving threats to the United States. Accordingly, DHS has a wide variety of needs as they relate to data to understand the threats. These needs include specific details on incident types, such as weapons used, as well as offender characteristics. To delineate these needs, we developed conceptual domains based on the DHS strategic framework and other policy documents. These domains assisted us in identifying gaps in existing databases in the upcoming chapters. We have also documented in this chapter that specific data needs or requirements are not always clear or consistent. However, documents and legislation strongly convey the need to understand threats from both strategic and tactical standpoints.

Figure 2.1
Framework for the Risk Assessment Methodology to Inform the Homeland Security National Risk Characterization

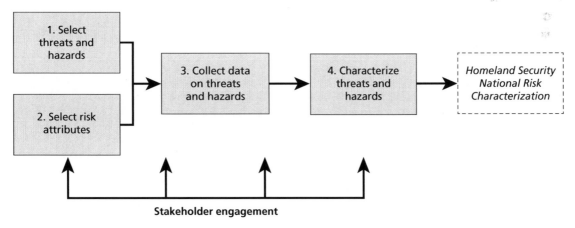

SOURCE: Willis et al., 2018, p. x.

CHAPTER THREE

The Current State of Databases on Terrorism and Targeted Violence

HSOAC researchers conducted a review of publicly available unclassified databases on terrorism and targeted violence to assess the alignment with DHS needs to understand rapidly evolving threats. We reviewed citations in academic and government studies and analysis and selected a subset of identified databases based on the time frame covered, frequency of citations, number of incidents included, and representation of various threats across the domains of terrorism and targeted violence. This chapter describes the search process used to identify the databases, the method of selecting the prominent databases within the priority domains identified in the DHS strategic framework, and an assessment of the most-prominent unclassified databases within each domain.

The HSOAC team employed a four-step approach for identifying and reviewing databases on terrorism and targeted violence (Figure 3.1). In the first step, we reviewed published research guides and scholarly bibliographies on terrorism and targeted violence, as well as inventories of relevant databases. Among the research guides and scholarly bibliographies, we considered the following sources: Center for Homeland Defense and Security, undated b; Duncan and Schmid, 2011; Forest, 2004; Forest et al., 2006; Grossman, 2017; Homo, Jones, and Russell, 2004; Jongman, 2011; Naval Postgraduate School, 2021; Perliger, 2010; Terrorism Research Initiative, undated; Tinnes, 2013; and Tinnes, 2014. For inventories of relevant databases, we turned to the following: Bowie, 2012; Bowie, 2017; Bowie, 2018; Bowie, 2020; Bowie and Schmid, 2011; Gordon, 2004; Schmid and Jongman, 1988; and Sheehan, 2011.

In the second step, we conducted a review of more than 100 widely used research sources on terrorism and targeted violence across four types of scholarly institutions:

- field-leading peer-reviewed journals
- major centers in academia focused on terrorism and extremism
- relevant U.S. government departments and agencies
- nonpartisan think tanks, NGOs, and commercial intelligence providers.

Figure 3.1
Database Identification and Review

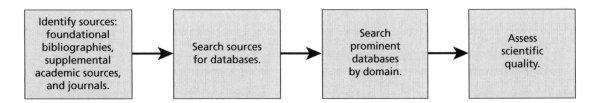

These research sources are summarized in Table 3.1.

Table 3.1
Key Sources Reviewed to Identify the Most-Prominent Databases

Category	Estimated Number	Key Examples
Peer-reviewed journals	35+	• *Behavioral Sciences of Terrorism and Political Aggression* • *Combating Terrorism Exchange* • *Counter Terrorism* • *Counter Terrorist Trends and Analyses* • *Criminal Justice and Behavior* • *Criminology* • *Criminology and Public Policy* • *Critical Studies on Terrorism* • *CTC Sentinel* • *Defence Against Terrorism Review* • *International Journal of Intelligence and Counterintelligence* • *Journal for Deradicalization* • *Journal of Conflict Resolution* • *Journal of Criminal Justice* • *Journal of Experimental Criminology* • *Journal of Peace Research* • *Journal of Policing, Intelligence and Counter Terrorism* • *Journal of Quantitative Criminology* • *Journal of Terrorism Research* • *Justice Quarterly* • *Law and Human Behavior* • *Perspectives on Terrorism* • *Studies in Conflict and Terrorism* • *Terrorism and Political Violence*
Academia	30+	• Belfer Center for Science and International Affairs, Harvard Kennedy School • Center for International Security and Cooperation, Stanford University • Center on Terrorism, Extremism, and Counterterrorism, Middlebury Institute of International Studies • Centre for Analysis of the Radical Right • Centre for Terrorism and Counterterrorism, University of Leiden • Dataverse, Harvard University • Empirical Studies of Conflict, Princeton University • Global Terrorism Research Project, Haverford College • GW Program on Extremism • Handa Centre for the Study of Terrorism and Political Violence, University of St. Andrews • Hoover Institution, Stanford University • ICPSR, University of Michigan • Institute for Security Policy and Law, Syracuse University • International Center for the Study of Terrorism, Pennsylvania State University • Josef Korbel School of International Studies, University of Denver • Triangle Center on Terrorism and Homeland Security, Duke University
U.S. government	15+	• Bureau of Counterterrorism, U.S. Department of State • Central Intelligence Agency • CTC, U.S. Military Academy at West Point • DHS • FBI • Naval Postgraduate School • NCTC • North Atlantic Treaty Organization centers of excellence • Strategic Studies Institute, U.S. Army War College • U.S. Department of Education • U.S. Department of Justice • U.S. Department of Labor • U.S. Department of the Treasury

Table 3.1—Continued

Category	Estimated Number	Key Examples
Think tanks, NGOs, and commercial intelligence	40+	• American Enterprise Institute • Anti-Defamation League • Atlantic Council • Brookings Institution • Carnegie Endowment for International Peace • Center for a New American Security • Center for Naval Analyses • Center for Strategic and International Studies • Chatham House • Council on Foreign Relations • Foreign Policy Research Institute • French Institute of International Relations • George C. Marshall European Center for Security Studies • Henry Jackson Society • Henry L. Stimson Center • Heritage Foundation • Hudson Institute • Institute for the Study of War • International Crisis Group • International Institute for Strategic Studies • Investigative Project on Terror • Jamestown Foundation • Janes • Konrad Adenauer Foundation • Middle East Institute • Middle East Media Research Institute • New America • Peace Research Institute Oslo • RAND Corporation • Royal United Services Institute • Search for International Terrorist Entities Intelligence Group • Soufan Group • Southern Poverty Law Center • Stiftung Wissenschaft und Politik • Stockholm International Peace Research Institute • U.S. Institute of Peace • Washington Institute for Near East Policy • Wilson Center

NOTE: NCTC = National Counterterrorism Center. CTC = Combating Terrorism Center. ICPSR = Inter-University Consortium for Political and Social Research.

Our search process yielded 137 databases that could be used to examine terrorism and targeted violence.[1] Table 3.2 provides summary statistics for these databases. Nearly two-thirds of the databases identified were dedicated to terrorism only (64%), while a smaller share was dedicated to targeted violence (15%) or to both terrorism and targeted violence (20%). Most of the databases (80%) included the United States, and 45% of the databases covered the entire world. Finally, incident-level databases were about twice as common as individual-level databases, and even more than that for other types.

In the third step, we identified the most-prominent databases by domain. Although we identified a large number of possible databases (137), we limited the subsequent analysis to only those databases that could readily be analyzed to understand and prevent current threats

---

[1] A full list of the databases can be found in Appendix A.

Table 3.2
Database Descriptive Statistics

Variable	Coding	Databases	Percentage
Subject coverage	Terrorism (only)	88	64
	Targeted violence (only)	21	15
	Both	28	20
	Total	137	100
Geographic coverage	Worldwide	62	45
	United States (only)	45	33
	United States and select other countries	2	1
	Non–United States	28	20
	Total	137	100
Temporal coverage	Pre-1960s	13	—
	1960s	24	—
	1970s	37	—
	1980s	50	—
	1990s	68	—
	2000s	92	—
	2010s	107	—
	Undetermined period[a]	22	—
Unit of observation[b]	Incidents	72	—
	Attack or target-type specific	9	—
	Individuals (including legal case focused)	35	—
	Groups and networks	27	—
	Government actions or policies	15	—
	Other or unknown	22	—
	Total	—	—

NOTE: Percentages do not sum to 100 because of rounding.

[a] Coverage dates could not be determined for 22 databases.

[b] Percentages are not provided here because some databases include multiple levels of observation.

of terrorism and targeted violence.[2] We thus narrowed the original list to 71 qualified databases that met five additional parameters:

---

[2] Our initial search efforts revealed more than 300 data sources. However, many of them were narrowly focused on testing a specific hypothesis rather than building an analytic tool that could be applied to a wider range of questions. Future efforts could benefit from a closer review of the original set of more than 300.

- They could be used for ongoing analysis by DHS.
- They were current through at least 2018.
- They included cases with direct relevance to the United States.
- They were not classified.
- They were readily available and could be readily analyzed.

We then identified the most prominent of these 71 qualified databases through a Scopus keyword search of the references and abstract fields to count the number of times each database was cited in the published literature. We then sorted the databases into relevant domains (see Chapter Two) and listed the databases with the most citations.

The results of this search by domain are presented in Table 3.3. In order to limit the breadth of our review and expedite the report, we selected the 10 most-prominent databases

Table 3.3
Selection of Prominent Databases Using Scopus Citation Counts

Database Name	Description	Scopus Counts
Transnational terrorism		
GTD	Global, 1970–2019, automated search, manual search, coding of media sources	1,538
PTS	Global, 1976–2018, manual coding of primary-source reports	646
UCDP Non-State Conflict Dataset	Global, 1975–2019, automated search, manual search, and code of media sources	154
IPT Court Cases database	Global, 2006–2021, manual search and coding of court cases	142
Extremist violence in the United States		
UCR Program data on hate crimes (FBI)	United States, 1995–2019, coded by responding officer	277
ECDB	United States, 1990–2018, automated search, manual search, and coding of media sources	91
Targeted violence		
UCDP GED	Global, 1989–2019, automated search, manual search, and coding of media sources	327
US Mass Shootings Database, 1982–2020	United States, 1982–2020, manual coding of media sources	212
School shootings		
K–12 School Shooting Database	United States, 1970–2018, compilation of existing data and manual verification with online sources	25
Washington Post School Shooting Database	United States, 1999–2018, manual coding of media sources	8

NOTE: PTS = Political Terror Scale. UCDP = Uppsala Conflict Data Program. IPT = Investigative Project on Terrorism. UCR = Uniform Crime Reporting. ECDB = Extremist Crime Database. GED = Georeferenced Event Dataset. Our review of the sources on terrorism and targeted violence identified no unclassified databases on cyberthreats, suggesting the need for a modified search process.

(most cited) for detailed review: the top four from transnational terrorism and the top two each from extremist violence, targeted violence, and school shootings.[3]

In the fourth step, we reviewed the quality-control techniques of the 10 most prominent databases (see Table 3.3) to determine whether each database's creation followed a transparent data collection process that could be replicated based on the description of the process in the project codebook, website, or other method documentation. Also, we assessed the rigor of the data collection process, checking for quality controls, potential sources of coding bias, and internal validity checks. We used a scoring sheet with 39 quality dimensions designed to assess the fitness of the databases for DHS data needs (see Appendix C).

Our quality-control review was informed by R. Wang and Strong, 1996, and Strong, Lee, and Wang, 1997, focusing on the aspects of contextual and accessible data quality. We understand that many attributes of databases can be analyzed to rate data quality; parts of R. Wang and Strong's framework discussing intrinsic data quality and accessibility data quality were appropriate for this analysis (R. Wang and Strong, 1996). Further, because this project was centered on publicly available databases, Mayernik's model considers transparency and accountability of open data (Mayernik, 2017), and questions in our coding schema represent this. This is evident, for example, in our questions related to coding manuals. The methodology was also guided by Brackstone, 1999, in that our selection of databases was guided by relevance and accessibility of data sets, and our process in this chapter assesses additional characteristics of accessibility and interpretability. We also understand that *quality* is not an easy term to define for data (Brackstone, 1999), but our analysis provides an initial assessment of one indicator of quality in widely cited databases on terrorism and targeted violence. Although we did not have the resources to analyze and manipulate data within the individual databases, we focused on accessibility and intrinsic data quality as represented in Appendix C. Intrinsic data quality consists of the following dimensions: accuracy, objectivity, believability, and reputation. Accessibility and access security (which includes restricted data access) are dimensions that make up accessibility data quality (Strong, Lee, and Wang, 1997; R. Wang and Strong, 1996).

We coded each of the databases for the 39 fields described in Appendix C. The 39 fields were selected to determine the fitness of the collected data for DHS data needs. Due to project resource constraints, we limited our review to only the information contained in the readily available documentation, usually codebooks and websites. Also, we used a very simple and inclusive coding process because most of the documentation did not explicitly address the quality fields. Our simple coding process credited a database with a "yes" if any evidence of the quality condition was found in the study documentation. For example, if the documentation did not describe a *double-coding* process but indicated that incongruent cases were adjudicated between the primary and secondary coders, we considered the *double-coding* condition satisfied. It is likely that relying only on the documentation understated the quality score while our inclusive coding overstated the score.

We believe that a more detailed and accurate quality score could be produced if we had access to internal study documentation and the resources to interview the database principal investigators and data collection staff. This better source information could be scored with

---

[3]   A description of each of the 10 selected databases can be found in Appendix B.

a more discerning coding process (e.g., clearly documented in codebook, conducted but not clearly documented, conducted informally but not documented).

Using this simple coding process, we were able to characterize the level of data collection quality in the 10 most-prominent databases within the key domains. Table 3.4 shows that the leading unclassified databases attempted to adhere to common documentation standards and transparency. All the reviewed databases clearly defined their study populations, most provided a codebook or other documentation, most clearly defined their sources and process, and most shared their sources of funding in the documentation.

Although most of the databases provided some form of documentation, the contents and format of the documentation were highly variable and inconsistently provided. Some provided codebooks and supporting materials on a public-facing website, some summarized their data collection methods in the body of a website, and some required contact with the study team to secure copies of the materials. Some of the codebooks were longer than 100 pages; others were just a few pages or even a few paragraphs on a website. This could be a concern because variability in the documentation process could increase the chance that a data user will misinterpret the data and increase the difficulty for the user to verify the level of rigor in the data collection process.

Table 3.4
Assessment Data Collection Process Using Database Documentation

Characteristic	Databases
Study population is clearly defined	10
Codebook or similar documentation is available on the website or on request	9
Primary sources for coding case details are clearly identified	8
Funding sources are clearly identified	8
Clear process exists for challenging coding decisions	7
Source of frame elements (cases or events) is clearly defined	7
Documentation is sufficient to replicate the frame	6
Coders' background is identified (e.g., students, professional coders, interns)	6
Adjudication process for coding exists	6
A coding form, manual, and data-entry system is used	6
Size of the coding team is reported	6
Documented quality-control process exists	6
Cases are double coded	5
Coding notes for cases are provided in documentation	5
Document indicates a formal training process for coders	4
Advisory board for coding rules exists	2
Recruiting process for coders is described	1
Formal vetting process for cases by scientific community exists	0

NOTE: $n = 10$.

Table 3.4 also shows that some components of data quality were infrequently reported. For example, only about half of the databases' documentation provided information about the characteristics of their coders, described an adjudication process, indicated that the coding used a formal manual or data-entry software, or had a documented quality-control process. Also, only half reported that they double-coded cases, and only half reported the available notes about the coding decisions. Perhaps most surprising, only four of the 10 indicated that they used a formal training process for their coders, and only one provided a description about how coders were recruited. This might be pernicious, considering that all the databases reported at least some level of manual coding that could be affected by the abilities of the people scoring the data.

An alternative explanation of the findings in Table 3.4 is that the investigators for each study employed the quality standards listed in Appendix C but did not report them in their study documentation, at least not in the readily available documentation reviewed in this study. This is likely true for many of the fields, such as "coders' background is clearly identified," because it is reasonable to assume that the investigators would know the demographic characteristics of their coders. However, it has been shown that the characteristics of the staff collecting the data (coders) can have an impact on the measures in the reported data (K. Wang, Kott, and Moore, 2013). The exclusion of this information from the documentation prevents the data user from assessing the impact that coder characteristics could have on the reported data. The investigators should not only note the characteristics of the coders but also include an assessment of the relationship between basic demographic information about the coders and key outcome measures. This issue should be addressed in future studies through an examination of all related study materials and interviews with the investigators, leading eventually to better standards in both quality control and study documentation.

Conclusions

The review of the available data was generally encouraging. The data collection community has generated a tremendous amount of unclassified and readily available data that can be used to understand terrorism and targeted violence. Our search showed that 137 usable databases are available and that 71 of these could readily be applied to DHS needs, with multiple databases to cover four of the five domains identified in the DHS strategic framework.

Less encouraging is that the cybersecurity domain was not covered in the readily available unclassified data. This is likely an artifact of the scope of our analysis and the types of databases we examined. By focusing on publicly available unclassified databases, we did not capture classified databases or commercial products that could measure timely emerging issues, such as cyberthreats. Publicly available unclassified databases are more likely to be delayed by the lag between the identification of a policy need and the dissemination of the database. This lag can be caused by the time required for the data collection community to secure funding, build, and publish the public databases.

Also less encouraging are the documentation and data quality standards. Although the 10 most-prominent databases demonstrated an attempt at rigor and transparency, it is concerning that not all provided codebooks or similar documentation; that the codebooks were all different; that some required direct contact with the research team to be granted access to the codebook; and that many of the prominent databases did not clearly report information that would be needed to replicate their efforts. Our review shows a gap between the documented quality, transparency, and rigor required for end users to have confidence in data used to study terrorism and targeted violence. This gap is likely a product of both inconsistent documentation processes and nonstandard quality-control procedures, which can be addressed through more-explicit expectations or requirements from the data user community.

CHAPTER FOUR

Conclusions and Recommendations

The objective of this study was to identify the set of publicly available unclassified databases, compare them with DHS needs, and highlight gaps that can be addressed through additional programmatic and research activities to help understand rapidly evolving threats. In this chapter, we compare the documented DHS data needs that were identified in Chapter Two with the publicly available unclassified databases identified in Chapter Three. Through this comparison, we identify gaps in the data coverage and make recommendations for improving sources of data, integration of data, and standardization of data.

This chapter considers the challenges and benefits of various options, including maintaining existing databases, improving existing databases, and initiating a new database development effort. This chapter also provides recommendations for improving the overall quality of data generated by the research community, as well as process changes that could help better meet DHS data needs.

Gap Analysis

Table 4.1 provides a summary of the data needs identified in the DHS strategic framework and other supporting documents as summarized in Tables 2.1 through 2.7 in Chapter Two. These data requirements are compared with the current state of available unclassified data on terrorism and targeted violence to identify gaps and, where possible, suggest improvements through high-priority actions.

Recommendations for Meeting Data Needs

The gap analysis indicates four opportunities for DHS to improve the evidence-based study of terrorism and targeted violence:

- First, fund continued updates and maintenance to the prominent databases, and take opportunities to support new data construction, where needed, and alignment with prominent databases on terrorism and targeted violence, where appropriate, to cover apparent data needs for emerging areas, such as cyberthreats or new technologies.
- Second, require any DHS-supported study to uniformly apply quality and transparency standards across the prominent databases. The current, nonuniform application of such

Table 4.1
Gaps in Unclassified Data to Meet Needs Documented in the DHS Strategic Framework and Secondary Sources

Data Need	Gaps	Recommended Priority Actions
Coverage of the five priority domains		
• Terrorism • Violent extremism • Targeted violence • Cyberthreats • School shootings	• Multiple options apparent for each domain except cyber. • Requirements are emerging for additional priority domains. • Requirements are emerging for more auxiliary fields in priority domains.	• Expand review to more thoroughly examine available cyberthreat data, consider needs for new unclassified databases on cyberthreats, and align existing cyberthreat data with prominent databases on terrorism and targeted violence. • Initiate new-database construction for additional high-priority domains. • Update prominent databases with additional auxiliary fields.
Data quality		
• Valid • Reliable	• Data quality is variable among prominent databases. • Even high-quality databases are not uniformly documented across the discipline. • Documentation is not always readily available. • Quality control is inconsistently applied. • No routine validation exists. • No clear standards exist for documentation or quality control for relevant data.	• Develop clear standards for all DHS-funded data, promulgated at the pre-award stage. • Provide guidance and support for external validation or self-validation. • Engage with a standards organization or professional association to define expectations. • Provide clear expectations for documentation.
Temporal coverage		
• Historical • Current	• Older databases provide valuable historical context but are often not maintained and current. • Automated data collection methods can provide timelier data, but quality assurance and analysis of files require more time and resources.	• Develop methods and funding for just-in-time updates to prominent databases on key outcome measures. • Provide just-in-time data requirements from DHS leadership that reflect emerging DHS needs on key outcome measures. • Set clear expectations about frequency of updates. • Set up rapid-response teams for amendments to search and inclusion criteria. • Review and update, as appropriate, older discontinued data sets that might contain information relevant to emerging policy needs.
Emerging threats and policy needs[a]		
• Unmanned aircraft systems • E-commerce • Media messages • Other emergent needs	• Databases do not include required outcome and auxiliary measures for emerging topics. • The wide variety of emerging threats requires a down-selecting process.	• Develop methods and funding for just-in-time new-database construction. • Prioritize emerging issues.

Table 4.1—Continued

Data Need	Gaps	Recommended Priority Actions
Program effectiveness		
• Program evaluations • After-action reports • Lessons learned • Best practices • Preparedness measures	• Effectiveness requires the integration of the outcome measures from the violence data with the performance measures collected at the program level. • Program-level requirements need to be included in the design of the violence databases.	• Guidelines are needed from the programs about intended use of the outcome measures for analytic relevance, including identifying evaluation time periods (pre and post) and geographic analysis levels. • A new-build or merging exercise is needed with program data.
Mission-driven data needs		
• All hazards • Illicit border crossing • Transportation • Immigration • Maritime nonstate threats • WMD • CBRN • Urban-area threats • Local threats • Risk assessments	• Each mission requirement will use different auxiliary measures. • Each mission might require different outcome measures from other missions.	• Inventory the available databases by mission area. • Update or create new-database construction as needed.

standards indicates an opportunity for DHS to clarify its expectations and potentially lead the discipline toward better standards of data collection.

- Third, invest in new data collection methods and an expedited process for identifying new data needs, and identify funding efforts to address these needs. Meeting DHS analytic needs requires, in many cases, timely data and novel measures of program effectiveness for counterterrorism. DHS can improve data's timeliness and relevance to emerging issues and program evaluations through this combination of actions.

- Finally, continue research in this area. This study was designed as a very limited–scope rapid initial assessment of databases in the public domain. Future studies could provide a more thorough assessment of the challenges of aligning data collection efforts to DHS needs.

In this section, we expand on each of these recommendations.

Make Continued Updates and New-Database Construction

As shown in Table 3.2 in Chapter Three, a large number of publicly available unclassified databases (137) can be used to support DHS data needs. However, there might be a need for the construction of a new unclassified database for cyberthreats, as noted in Table 3.3. Although cyber was identified in the DHS strategic framework as one of the key domains, we found no current unclassified cyberthreat databases in our search.[1] This is presumably a function of our search process, which was unlikely to identify database fields outside the literature on terrorism and targeted violence and newer data collection efforts that have not been reported in that

---

[1] Our initial search process did not reveal a cyberthreat database. However, during the review stage, we identified the Significant Cyber Incidents timeline, which is a well-known source in the cyber community (Center for Strategic and International Studies, undated). This late discovery demonstrates the limits to our search process and the need for an expanded search process in future studies. It is likely that our rapid initial assessment process excluded other relevant databases because of our limiting assumptions.

literature. This demonstrates the complexity of the DHS data needs, which extend beyond a single body of literature and highlights the importance of more-extensive research on meeting DHS data needs. Our focus on only unclassified publicly available data was a design decision intended to reduce the scope to meet the abbreviated schedule.

There is also a need for data on emerging technology threats, such as unmanned aircraft systems, emerging issues, and new policy requirements. The needs for new data can be met through the construction of new databases on those topics. There is also a need for continued updates to existing databases, to keep their information current by adding cases as events develop. These databases should be updated with auxiliary data that measure the use of emerging technologies and time impact on outcomes, such as terrorism or extremism. Continued updates will keep the data current and will allow researchers to leverage historical data for trend analysis to better understand the context of emerging issues. The existing databases can also be used to meet the program evaluation needs of DHS components through the merging of administrative records about program activities and collection of new data relevant to specific program objectives.

The construction of new databases to satisfy current unmet needs is likely to be time-consuming, expensive, and risky if the threat environment and policy needs change. However, for some high-priority needs, potentially including cybersecurity, the investment is likely justified because of the considerable need to understand the threat and because of the absence of unclassified data to meet the demand. For the studies it funds or supports, DHS can manage the costs and risks of new-database construction by leveraging the inventory of existing databases with continued updates and through periodic prioritization and revision of the data requirements identified in the DHS strategic framework. Our initial search identified a large number of single-use data collections designed for testing specific hypotheses. These single-use studies might have potential to address current policy needs and might provide value once updated.

Uniformly Apply Standards for Data Quality and Transparency
The observed level of quality in the 10 prominent databases reviewed in Chapter Three was adequate and showed a commitment by the research teams to rigor and transparency. However, some of the quality-control measures were not clearly addressed in study documentation and could be addressed through future updates, included in requirements for DHS-funded new-database construction, or as recommended standards to clarify DHS expectations. These include clear standards for quality control and documentation promulgated by DHS at the design (preaward) stage. These standards would promote transparency, consistency, and quality in the databases, and the establishment of standards would allow research teams to plan accordingly. Many federal agencies have established and promulgated standards for data collection to guide their constituent research communities (see Table 4.2 for some examples). The use of standards does not mean that all databases have the same content or intended use; rather, it means that the data collection community has a set of guidelines that members can use to design their data collection programs, as well as a clear set of expectations for how they manage and report the quality-control process.

As part of these standards, DHS can include requirements for the contents and format of study documentation, the frequency of documentation updates for ongoing studies, the expectation that all documents be readily available, and a clear process for questioning or challenging coding rules and decisions. Study documentation and database structure are crucial com-

Table 4.2
Examples of Federal Data Requirements to Promote Consistency and Quality Across Databases

Agency	Data Requirement Guidance	Reference or Source	Consideration
U.S. Food and Drug Administration	Standard-based submission with support from a standards organization	"CDISC Standards in the Clinical Research Process" (Clinical Data Interchange Standards Consortium, undated)	Maintaining a standards organization is time-consuming but puts the burden on industry for compliance.
National Institute of Justice	Requires that any submission use a structured format	"National Archive of Criminal Justice Data" (National Institute of Corrections, undated)	The archive allows the data submission requirement to enforce compliance but puts the burden on the archive to verify compliance with conditions.
Office of the Assistant Secretary for Planning and Evaluation, U.S. Department of Health and Human Services	Uniform data collection standards for surveys under the Patient Protection and Affordable Care Act	"U.S. Department of Health and Human Services Implementation Guidance on Data Collection Standards for Race, Ethnicity, Sex, Primary Language, and Disability Status" (Office of the Assistant Secretary for Planning and Evaluation, 2011)	The guidance document is specific to agency needs but can require frequent updates and places the burden for compliance verification on the agency.

ponents for a transparent research process and can facilitate improvements, revisions, updates, and additions to the current databases from the data user community.

Finally, the quality of the data collection process could be improved through the application of a validation process. Some of the databases reviewed already use a simple self-validation process of comparing their coded values with those reported in other databases. This is a valuable addition and should be encouraged in all new databases, but it is limited to those cases that are duplicated in other sources. A more comprehensive approach is to subsample the collected cases and use an independent review to replicate those cases. This process could be completed by the data collection team as part of the self-validation, or DHS could use a third-party validation organization. Validation can be time-consuming and expensive, so any requirements should be carefully considered and developed in coordination with the data collection teams. Again, like with the other standards, it is very important that the validation process be shared before the data collection plan is developed and that the validation method be standardized and reported as part of data collection documentation.

Invest in New Data Collection Methods

The DHS strategic framework identifies two classes of needs that can be addressed through the development of new methods: rapid updates and program effectiveness. The rapid updating requirement stems from the need to quickly analyze the changing threat environment and recent events within analytic frameworks established with the existing databases. The existing documentation showed that many of the databases reviewed in Chapter Four had at least a one-year lag in the availability of the public analytic file. This lag could be reduced through the development of new techniques for case identification and reporting. Four of the 10 databases reviewed in Chapter Four are already using an automated process for identifying new cases, so rapid inclusion of new cases and (perhaps) new fields is possible without creating new methods. However, it is likely that the one-year lag is not a function of the harvesting of cases from the primary sources but rather a function of the time required for quality control, public dissemination, and the pace of the government funding cycle. Although we do not recommend reducing the time spent on quality control, preliminary analytic files can be made available for review to address priority policy requirements while quality checks are being implemented. DHS can also improve the currency of the data through expedited data requirement reporting and just-in-time contract vehicles.

Considerations for Future Research

We employed a rapid initial assessment process to produce a report on DHS data needs in less than 90 days. The objective was to quickly highlight broad gaps in the available data so that new programmatic and research needs could be identified to help address rapidly evolving threats. To meet this objective, we limited the scope by

- relying primarily on the DHS strategic framework to identify DHS database needs, augmented with supplementary strategic and related documents
- scheduling only very limited engagement with the creators and consumers of the relevant data
- limiting our data review to the readily available, unclassified published databases through searches of websites and the published literature
- limiting our quality review to the small subset (10) of the most-cited databases and conducting a quality assessment using only the published methodological materials
- limiting our recommendations to only those gaps that could be identified with this rapid process, noting areas that could be expanded for improved decisionmaking through future research.

Although our design was effective in streamlining the research process, some of our decisions prevented us from exploring all the lines of investigation that might inform DHS needs. Through the implementation of the study, we identified several enhancements for future studies that could improve our understanding of these issues:

- We limited our study to unclassified, readily available, and highly cited (prominent) databases. It is likely that this excluded databases that might have satisfied some of the needs from the DHS strategic framework. A future study should include classified and commercial data as appropriate.
- Our quality assessment was based on the study documentation (e.g., codebooks, method articles). However, the completeness of these documents varied considerably. The research teams might have included the quality conditions but not considered it necessary to include an explanation in the documentation. We believe that interviews with the research teams could improve the accuracy of the quality assessments and would help us develop guidelines for documentation standards.
- Our review of the DHS data needs was limited to only the DHS strategic framework and related documentation. These documents covered a much broader topic area than data collection needs, resulting in an overly general set of identified data needs. A more thor-

ough and specific set of data needs could be generated through a series of interviews with data users from the DHS components and academic end users.

- Our review of the contents of each of the databases was limited to simple classification. A more detailed review of the contents of the databases should be conducted to better understand the alignment with the more-specific DHS requirements that could be produced through interviews with the DHS data users.
- We reviewed a small number (10) of the total number of possible databases that could be used for terrorism and targeted violence. A larger and more representative set of databases would provide a better description of the state of the data on terrorism and targeted violence.
- Our quality check was limited to a review of the study documentation. A more rigorous check could include validation against external sources, detailed review of a sample of cases, or replication of a sample of cases. For example, GTD documented significant changes to the data collection design as the study migrated through different hosting organizations. A more rigorous review of the documentation, combined with interviews with investigators might reveal similar, but undocumented, changes in other databases.
- Our search and identification efforts identified nearly 300 data collections that addressed topics related to terrorism and targeted violence. However, to reduce the scope, we excluded data collections that were designed as single-use files to test specific questions or summarize a finite series of events. We recognize that this reduction might have excluded valuable data collections that, with some investment, could be updated and used to fulfill DHS needs across the domains.

A more rigorous follow-up study could also develop several knowledge products that DHS could provide to the data collection community to improve the overall quality of DHS-sponsored databases. This could include an expansion of Table 4.2 to identify agency guidance provided to other federal data collections in an attempt to standardize within DHS efforts and to align with other agencies. DHS could also produce a set of standards for quality and documentation that must be met for any data collection effort either to receive DHS funds or to be used for DHS analysis. Such standards could be promulgated prior to the funding process so that investigators can design appropriate studies. As part of the standardization, DHS could provide the requirements for a self-validation process for databases. Such a process could provide the guidelines for sampling the databases, conducting validation against external sources, and examining likely sources of bias and error caused by the data collection process.

Databases Identified

In Table A.1, we list the 137 databases we identified and their sources or hosts.

Table A.1
Databases Identified

Host	Database
Action on Armed Violence	Explosive Violence Monitor (Action on Armed Violence, undated)
African Centre for the Study and Research on Terrorism	Database on terrorism and the Africa Terrorism Bulletin (African Centre for the Study and Research on Terrorism, 2019)
Anti-Defamation League (ADL) Center on Extremism	Hate Crime Map (ADL Center on Extremism, undated a)
	Hate, Extremism, Antisemitism, Terrorism Map (ADL Center on Extremism, undated b)
	Tracker of Antisemitic Incidents (ADL Center on Extremism, undated c)
Armed Conflict Location and Event Data Project (ACLED)	ACLED database (ACLED, undated)
	Pilot project on U.S. political violence and demonstrations (Kishi and Carboni, 2019)
Aviation Safety Network (ASN)	ASN Safety Database (Flight Safety Foundation, 2021)
B'Tselem	B'Tselem statistical data sets (B'Tselem, undated)
British Broadcasting Corporation (BBC)	BBC News Database of UK Jihadists (BBC, 2017)
Bureau of Investigative Journalism	Drone Warfare (Bureau of Investigative Journalism, undated)
Canadian Global Security	Counter-Terrorism Initiatives (African Union) Resources Database
Canadian Network for Research on Terrorism, Security and Society	Canadian Incident Database (Canadian Network for Research on Terrorism, Security and Society, undated)
Center for Homeland Defense and Security, Naval Postgraduate School	K–12 School Shooting Database (Center for Homeland Defense and Security, undated a)
Center for International Security and Cooperation, Stanford University	Mapping Militants Project (Center for International Security and Cooperation, undated)
Center for Research on Extremism, Faculty of Social Sciences, University of Oslo	Right-Wing Terrorism and Violence data set, western Europe (Ravndal, 2016)

Table A.1—Continued

Host	Database
Center for Terrorism and Intelligence Studies	Critical Infrastructure Terrorist Attack (Center for Terrorism and Intelligence Studies, undated)
Center on Terrorism, Extremism, and Counterterrorism; Middlebury Institute of International Studies	Special Operations Research Database (Center on Terrorism, Extremism, and Counterterrorism, undated)
Centers for Disease Control and Prevention	School-Associated Violent Death Surveillance System (Centers for Disease Control and Prevention, 2019)
	Web-Based Injury Statistics Query and Reporting System (Centers for Disease Control and Prevention, 2020)
Centre for Analysis of the Radical Right and University of North Carolina	Racially and Ethnically Motivated Violent Extremism (Mattheis et al., 2020)
Centre for Defence and International Security Studies Terrorism Programme, Lancaster University	Terrorist Incidents 1945 to 1998
Centre for Terrorism and Counterterrorism, Leiden University	Terrorism, Counterterrorism and Radicalization (Centre for Terrorism and Counterterrorism, undated)
Chicago Project on Security and Threats, University of Chicago	Suicide Attack Database (Chicago Project on Security and Threats, undated)
Combating Terrorism Center at West Point (CTC)	Harmony Program (CTC, undated)
Communities Against Hate	"Hate Magnified: Communities in Crisis" (Leadership Conference Education Fund, undated)
Congo Research Group, Center on International Cooperation, New York University and Human Rights Watch	Kivu Security Tracker (Kivu Security Tracker, undated)
Council on Foreign Relations	Global Conflict Tracker (Council on Foreign Relations, 2021b)
	Nigeria Security Tracker (Council on Foreign Relations, 2021a)
Counter Extremism Project	Extremist Groups Database (Counter Extremism Project, undated a)
	Terrorists and Extremists Database (Counter Extremism Project, undated b)
EBSCO Information Services	International Security and Counter-Terrorism Reference Center (EBSCO Information Services, undated)
Education Week	School Shooting Tracker (Maxwell, Peele, and Superville, 2021)
Esri Story Maps and Peace Tech Lab	Esri Story Maps on terrorist attacks (Bock, 2020)
European Union Agency for Criminal Justice Cooperation (Eurojust)	Counter-Terrorism Register (Eurojust, 2019)
Europol	European Union Terrorism Situation and Trend Report (Europol, undated)
Everytown for Gun Safety	EveryStat (EveryStat, undated)
	"Gunfire on School Grounds in the United States" (Everytown Research and Policy, undated)
Federal Bureau of Investigation (FBI)	UCR Program data on hate crimes (Criminal Justice Information Services, undated)

Table A.1—Continued

Host	Database
Foreign Fighter Project	Foreign Fighter Project, 1815–2015 (Malet, undated)
George Washington University (GW) Program on Extremism	Dollars for Daesh data set (Vidino, Lewis, and Mines, 2020)
	Extremism Tracker: ISIS [Islamic State of Iraq and Syria] in America (GW Program on Extremism, undated b)
	Extremism Tracker: ISIS legal cases (GW Program on Extremism, undated c)
	Attacks Tracker: Jihadist Motivated Terrorist Attacks in Europe and North America (GW Program on Extremism, undated a)
German Institute on Radicalization and De-Radicalization Studies	Database on Terrorism in Germany: Jihadism (German Institute on Radicalization and De-Radicalization Studies, 2021)
	Database on Terrorism in Germany: Right-Wing Extremism (German Institute on Radicalization and De-Radicalization Studies, 2021)
Gun Violence Archive	Mass Shootings (Gun Violence Archive, undated)
Hague Centre for Strategic Studies	Jihadist Foreign Fighters Monitor (Hague Centre for Strategic Studies, undated)
Heritage Foundation	Terrorist Plots Since 9/11 (Bucci, Carafano, and Zuckerman, 2013)
IHS Jane's	Insurgency and Terrorism Centre (Janes, undated)
Institute for Conflict Management	South Asia Terrorism Portal (Institute for Conflict Management, undated)
Institute for Security Studies	Comprehensive Database of African Counter-Terrorism Law and Policy (Institute for Security Studies, 2010)
Institute for the Study of Violent Groups, University of New Haven (now the Center for Analytics; formerly associated with Sam Houston State University)	Violent Extremism Knowledge Base (Institute for the Study of Violent Groups, undated)
Integrated Network for Societal Conflict Research, Center for Systemic Peace	High Casualty Terrorist Bombings (Integrated Network for Societal Conflict Research, undated)
IntelCenter	IntelCenter Database (IntelCenter, undated a)
	Terrorist Facial Recognition (IntelCenter, undated b)
Inter-University Consortium for Political and Social Research (ICPSR), University of Michigan; START (a DHS center of excellence); School of Criminal Justice, Michigan State University; and National Archive of Criminal Justice Data, University of Michigan	Terrorism and Preparedness Data Resource Center (START, undated c)
International Atomic Energy Agency	Incident and Trafficking Database (International Atomic Energy Agency, undated)
International Centre for Political Violence and Terrorism Research, S. Rajaratnam School of International Studies	Global Pathfinder Database (International Centre for Political Violence and Terrorism Research, undated)
International Institute for Counter-Terrorism	Incidents and Activists Database (International Institute for Counter-Terrorism, undated)

Table A.1—Continued

Host	Database
International Institute for Strategic Studies	Armed Conflict Database (International Institute for Strategic Studies, undated)
Investigative Project on Terrorism (IPT)	Court Cases (IPT, undated b)
	Terrorist groups and individuals (IPT, undated c)
James Martin Center for Nonproliferation Studies for the Nuclear Threat Initiative	Global Incidents and Trafficking Database (Meyer, Lengcher, and Oh, 2020)
James Martin Center for Nonproliferation Studies WMD Terrorism Research Program, Middlebury Institute of International Studies	Monterey WMD Terrorism Database (Monterey Terrorism Research and Education Program, undated)
Jewish Virtual Library, American–Israeli Cooperative Enterprise	Terrorism Against Israel Database (1920–present) (Jewish Virtual Library, undated)
John Jay College of Criminal Justice, City University of New York	John Jay and Artis Transnational Terrorism Database (John Jay and Artis Transnational Terrorism Database, undated)
John Jay College of Criminal Justice, City University of New York; Michigan State University; Seattle University; Indiana University–Purdue University Indianapolis; and START	ECDB (Freilich et al., 2014)
Long War Journal	US Airstrikes in the Long War ("US Airstrikes in the Long War," undated)
Mass Shooting Tracker	Database (Gun Violence Archive, undated)
Mineta Transportation Institute	Terrorist and Serious Criminal Attacks Against Public Surface Transportation (Mineta Transportation Institute, 2017)
Mother Jones	"US Mass Shootings, 1982–2021" (Follman, Aronsen, and Pan, 2021)
Mother Jones and the Investigative Reporting Program at the University of California, Berkeley	Mother Jones terrorism database
Muslim Public Affairs Council	Post-9/11 Terrorism Incident Database (Muslim Public Affairs Council, 2013)

Table A.1—Continued

Host	Database
National Consortium for the Study of Terrorism and Responses to Terrorism (START), University of Maryland	Bias Incidents and Actors Study (Bruza, 2020)
	GTD (START, undated b)
	Nuclear Facilities Attack Database (Ackerman and Halverson, undated)
	Profiles of Incidents Involving CBRN and Non-State Actors (Binder, undated)
	Profiles of Individual Radicalization in the United States (Yates et al., undated)
	Profiles of Perpetrators of Terrorism in the United States (Miller and Smarick, undated)
	Radiological and Nuclear Non-State Adversaries Database (Ackerman and Sorrell, undated)
	Terrorism and Extremist Violence in the United States (LaFree et al., undated)
	Terrorist and Extremist Organizations (Wilkenfeld and Rethemeyer, undated)
National Counter Terrorism Authority	National Counter Terrorism Database
National Counterterrorism Center (NCTC)	Worldwide Incidents Tracking System (Chapman, 2016)
National Memorial Institute for the Prevention of Terrorism	International Terrorism: Attributes of Terrorist Events (currently hosted by Vinyard Software) (International Terrorism, undated)
	Terrorism Knowledge Base (RAND Corporation, undated)
National Police Foundation	Averted School Violence Data Collection Platform (National Police Foundation, undated)
National School Safety and Security Services	School Associated Violent Deaths and School Shootings Database (National School Safety and Security Services, undated)
New America	America's Counterterrorism Wars (Bergen, Sterman, and Salyk-Virk, 2021)
	Terrorism in America After 9/11 (Bergen, Ford, et al., 2020)
Odhikar	Statistical Data Sets on Political Violence (Odhikar, undated)
Office of the National Coordinator of Terrorist Investigations, UK Home Office	Counter-Terrorism Statistics (Operation of Police Powers under the Terrorism Act 2000) (UK Home Office, 2021)
OODA Loop	Terror Attack Database (formerly hosted at www.terrorism.com)
Our World in Data, University of Oxford	Terrorism data (Ritchie et al., 2019)
Pak Institute for Peace Studies (PIPS)	PIPS Security Database (PIPS, undated)
Pakistan Institute for Conflict and Security Studies	Database of Anti-State Violence (Pakistan Institute for Conflict and Security Studies, undated)
Pinkerton Global Intelligence Services (PGIS)	PGIS database (LaFree and Dugan, 2007)

Table A.1—Continued

Host	Database
University of Arizona Artificial Intelligence Lab (in collaboration with Drexel University, the University of Virginia, the University of Texas at Dallas, and the University of Utah)	Dark Web Forum Database (Jihadi Social Media) (Chen, undated)
Purdue University and University of North Carolina at Asheville	PTS (PTS, undated)
RAND Corporation	RAND Database of Worldwide Terrorism Incidents (RAND Corporation, undated)
Risk Advisory and Aon	Terrorism Tracker (Aon, Continuum Economics, and Risk Advisory Group, undated)
Rockefeller College of Public Affairs and Policy, University at Albany, State University of New York	Hot Spots of Hate and Violence: US County Level Analysis of Factors Related to Hate Crimes and Terrorism (Project on Violent Conflict, undated)
Rockefeller College of Public Affairs and Policy, University at Albany, State University of New York; University of Arizona; and START	Terrorist Attributes to Network Connections (Project on Violent Conflict, undated)
Schoolshootingdatabase.com	Comprehensive Database of All Types of American School Shootings (1840–present day) (Laurine, undated)
Southern Poverty Law Center	Extremist Files (Southern Poverty Law Center, undated)
	Hate map (Southern Poverty Law Center, 2021)
Stanford University	Mass Shootings in America (Stanford Mass Shootings of America, undated)
Stockholm International Peace Research Institute	Arms embargo database (Stockholm International Peace Research Institute, undated)
	Global Registry of Violent Deaths (Stockholm International Peace Research Institute, 2020)
Strauss Center for International Security and Law	Social Conflict Analysis Database (Salehyan et al., 2012)
T. M. C. Asser Instituut	International Crimes Database, Foreign Fighters tab (International Crimes Database Project, undated)
Terrorism Research and Analysis Consortium	Terrorist Group and Activities Database (Terrorism Research and Analysis Consortium, undated)
Terrorism Research Center, University of Arkansas	American Terrorism Study (Terrorism Research Center, undated)
Triangle Center on Terrorism and Homeland Security, Duke University	Muslim-American Involvement with Violent Extremism (O'Brien, 2021)
Ulster University	Conflict Archive on the Internet (Conflict and Politics in Northern Ireland, 2021)
United Nations Office on Drugs and Crime	Anti-Money-Laundering International Database (International Money Laundering Information Network, undated a)
	Case Law Database (International Money Laundering Information Network, undated b)

Table A.1—Continued

Host	Database
University of Arkansas and ICPSR	Identity and Framing Theory, Precursor Activity, and the Radicalization Process, American Terrorism Study, 1972–2008 (quantitative) (Smith et al., undated)
	Identity and Framing Theory, Precursor Activity, and the Radicalization Process, American Terrorism Study, 1972–2008 (qualitative) (Smith et al., undated)
	Longevity of American Terrorists: Factors Affecting Sustainability (United States), 1980–2015 (Smith, 2019)
	Sequencing Terrorists' Precursor Behaviors: A Crime Specific Analysis, United States, 1980–2012 (Smith, 2018)
University of Maryland	Minorities at Risk database (Minorities at Risk Project, 2016)
University of Massachusetts Lowell, School of Criminology and Justice Studies	Right-wing extremist violent incidents ("UMass Professor Analyzes Far-Right Violence," 2020)
Uppsala Conflict Data Program (UCDP)	Actor Dataset (Pettersson and Öberg, 2021; UCDP, undated)
	Battle-Related Deaths Dataset (Pettersson and Öberg, 2021; UCDP, undated)
	Ethnic One-Sided Violence Dataset (Fjelde et al., 2019; UCDP, undated)
	GED (Pettersson and Öberg, 2021; Sundberg and Melander, 2013; UCDP, undated)
	Non-State Conflict Dataset (Pettersson and Öberg, 2021; Sundberg, Eck, and Kreutz, 2012; UCDP, undated)
	One-Sided Violence Dataset (Pettersson and Öberg, 2021; Eck and Hultman, 2007; UCDP, undated)
Uppsala Conflict Data Program (UCDP) and Peace Research Institute Oslo	Armed Conflict Dataset (Pettersson and Öberg, 2021; Gleditsch et al., 2002; UCDP, undated)
Verisk Maplecroft	Maplecroft Terrorism Index (Verisk Maplecroft, undated)
Vinyard Software	Data on Terrorist Suspects (Vinyard Software, undated)
Violence Project	Mass Shooter Database (Violence Project, undated)
Washington Institute for Near East Policy	Lebanese Hezbollah Select Worldwide Activities Interactive Map and Timeline (Levitt, 2020)
Washington Post	School shootings (Cox et al., 2021)

NOTE: n = 137. Citations in parentheses are for the sources themselves or information about them.

Databases Selected

Table B.1
Summary of Selected Databases, by Domain

Database	Description (from Owner Website)	Population	Number of Observations	Coverage Start Year
Transnational terrorism				
GTD	"The Global Terrorism Database (GTD) is an open-source database including information on domestic and international terrorist attacks around the world from 1970 through 2019, and now includes more than 200,000 cases. For each event, information is available on the date and location of the incident, the weapons used and nature of the target, the number of casualties, and—when identifiable—the identity of those responsible." (START, undated a)	Terrorist attacks (intentional acts or threats of violence by nonstate actors for sociopolitical ends)	200,000	1970
PTS	"The PTS measures levels of political violence and terror that a country experiences in a particular year based on a 5-level 'terror scale' originally developed by Freedom House. The data used in compiling this index comes from three different sources: the yearly country reports of Amnesty International, the U.S. State Department Country Reports on Human Rights Practices, and Human Rights Watch's World Reports." (PTS, undated)	Synthesis of data available for a given country in a given year (e.g., "Germany, 2005")	9,324	1976
UCDP Non-State Conflict Dataset	UCDP defines *nonstate conflict* as "the use of armed force between two organized armed groups, neither of which is the government of a state, which results in at least 25 battle-related deaths in a year" (von Uexkull and Pettersson, 2018, p. 2). Data are collected from global newswires, local news in relevant areas, and other secondary sources (e.g., other media, NGO reports) (UCDP, undated b).	Acts of lethal violence by organized groups of nonstate actors in a single location	1,271	1989
IPT Court Cases database[a]	IPT claims to be "the world's most comprehensive data center on radical Islamic terrorist groups." The criteria used to populate the data set are unclear, but available data include case names, locations, dates, and defendants' alleged terror group affiliations. The Court Cases database is one of several maintained by IPT (IPT, undated a).	Court cases on Islamic terrorism–related charges	606	2006

Table B.1—Continued

Database	Description (from Owner Website)	Population	Number of Observations	Coverage Start Year
Violent extremism in the United States				
UCR data on hate crimes	The FBI's UCR program began collecting data on hate crimes in 1990 to comply with a new congressional mandate. The Hate Crime Statistics program keeps information on offenses that responding officers flagged as reflecting an offender's bias on the basis of race, gender, gender identity, religion, disability, sexual orientation, or ethnicity. These incidents are reviewed by "second-level judgment officer/unit," and data are submitted to the FBI via the National Incident-Based Reporting System (NIBRS) or the Summary Reporting System (SRS) (UCR, undated).	Hate crime incidents reported by LE agencies in the United States	209,441	1991
ECDB	The ECDB "is compiled by researchers located at Michigan State University, John Jay College, Indiana University–Purdue University, Indianapolis, and Seattle University. The ECDB is a relational database that includes information on all publicly known violent and financial crimes committed in the United States by extremists associated with the Islamic State of Iraq and the Levant (ISIL), the violent Far Right (FR), and the Animal and Earth Liberation Fronts (ELF and ALF). The ECDB includes information on the incidents themselves, as well as their perpetrators, related organizations, and victims" (TEVUS Analyst Portal, undated).	Incidents of extremist violence and financial crimes, as well as their perpetrators, organizations, and victims	4,000	1990
Targeted violence				
UCDP GED	"This dataset is UCDP's most disaggregated dataset, covering individual events of organized violence (phenomena of lethal violence occurring at a given time and place). These events are sufficiently fine-grained to be geo-coded down to the level of individual villages, with temporal durations disaggregated to single, individual days." Data are collected from global newswires, local news in relevant areas, and other secondary sources (e.g., other media, NGO reports) (UCDP, undated b).	Incidents and events of lethal organized violence	225,385	1989
US Mass Shootings Database[a]	Mother Jones has hosted a data set on U.S. mass shootings since 1982 as part of its investigative reporting (Follman, Aronsen, and Pan, 2021).	Mass shootings, defined as public rampages in which identifiable lone shooters kill four or more people	119	1982
Cyberthreats				
—	No unclassified databases were identified through the search process.[b]		Not applicable	Not applicable

Table B.1—Continued

Database	Description (from Owner Website)	Population	Number of Observations	Coverage Start Year
School shootings				
K–12 School Shooting Database	"The K–12 School Shooting Database research project is a widely inclusive database that documents each and every instance a gun is brandished, is fired, or a bullet hits school property for any reason, regardless of the number of victims, time, day of the week." Data are given on date, location, shooter age, weapon type, and some coded descriptions of the situation in question (Center for Homeland Defense and Security, undated a).	School shootings, defined as "each and every instance a gun is brandished, is fired, or a bullet hits school property for any reason, regardless of the number of victims, time, day of the week"	1,636	1970
Washington Post School Shooting Database[a]	"The Washington Post spent a year determining how many children have been affected by school shootings, beyond just those killed or injured. To do that, reporters attempted to identify every act of gunfire at a primary or secondary school during school hours since the Columbine High massacre on April 20, 1999. Using Nexis, news articles, open-source databases, law enforcement reports, information from school websites and calls to schools and police departments, The Post reviewed more than 1,000 alleged incidents but counted only those that happened on campuses immediately before, during or just after classes." (Cox et al., 2021)	School shootings, defined as incidents of gunfire "on campuses immediately before, during or just after classes"	238	1999

[a] Does not have a clearly identified description on website or other documentation.

[b] Our initial search process did not identify a cyberthreat database. However, during the review stage, we identified the Significant Cyber Incidents timeline, which is a well-known source in the cyber community (Center for Strategic and International Studies, undated). This late discovery demonstrates the limits to our search process and the need for an expanded search process in future studies. It is likely that our rapid initial assessment process excluded other relevant database because of our limiting assumptions.

Scoring Fields for Self-Reported Quality-Control Measures

These are the fields we coded for our review of self-reported quality-control measures:

- Is the codebook readily available?
- Are other methods or study documentation readily available?
- What is the use of the other document?
- Is codebook or other document readily available?
- Is there a codebook update schedule?
- Is the population clearly defined?
- What is the population?
- Is the source of frame elements clearly identified?
- What is the primary source of frame elements?
- What is the secondary source of frame elements?
- Is the document sufficient to replicate the frame?
- Does the source build on a previous source for cases?
- If so, does the source use previous coded values?
- What is the coder population (e.g., graduate students, interns)?
- How are they recruited?
- How are they screened?
- Are they trained?
- Is there a coding manual?
- Is there a coding form?
- Are fields in the data dictionary (coded values) supported by an external source?
- What is the number of coders (small team, large team)?
- Is there a quality control process?
- Does quality control validate coded cases?
- Are cases double coded?
- Are cases double blind coded?
- Is there an adjudication process?
- Are there coding notes?
- Does the scientific community vet a sample of coded cases?
- Is there a users' association that reviews cases?
- Is there an advisory board that sets data collection rules?
- Is there an annual meeting of data users?
- Do they report intercoder reliability scores?
- Are the primary sources that are used to code case details clearly identified?

- What is the primary source used to code case details (e.g., location, victims)?
- What is the secondary source to code case details?
- Is there a validation process for the primary source?
- Is there a missing data protocol?
- How are they funded?
- Do users have a process to challenge coding decisions?

References

Ackerman, Gary A., and James Halverson, "Nuclear Facility Attack Database," National Consortium for the Study of Terrorism and Responses to Terrorism, undated. As of May 24, 2021:
https://www.start.umd.edu/data-tools/nuclear-facility-attack-database

Ackerman, Gary, and Maranda Sorrell, "Radiological and Nuclear Non-State Adversaries Database (RANNSAD)," National Consortium for the Study of Terrorism and Responses to Terrorism, undated. As of May 24, 2021:
https://www.start.umd.edu/data-tools/radiological-and-nuclear-non-state-adversaries-database-rannsad

ACLED—*See* Armed Conflict Location and Event Data Project.

Action on Armed Violence, "Explosive Violence Monthly Reports," undated. As of May 22, 2021:
https://aoav.org.uk/2019/monitoring-explosive-violence-in-2018/

ADL Center on Extremism—*See* Anti-Defamation League Center on Extremism.

African Centre for the Study and Research on Terrorism, "Africa Terrorism Bulletin," January 25, 2019. As of May 22, 2021:
https://caert.org.dz/africa-terrorism-bulletin/

Alathari, Lina, Ashley Blair, Diana Drysdale, Catherine Camilletti, Jeffrey McGarry, Steven Driscoll, and Amanda Snook, *Mass Attacks in Public Spaces, 2017*, Washington, D.C.: National Threat Assessment Center, U.S. Secret Service, U.S. Department of Homeland Security, March 2018. As of March 31, 2021:
https://www.secretservice.gov/sites/default/files/reports/2020-09/USSS_FY2017_MAPS.pdf

Alathari, Lina, Steven Driscoll, Ashley Blair, Diana Drysdale, Arna Carlock, and Jeffrey McGarry, *Mass Attacks in Public Spaces, 2018*, Washington, D.C.: National Threat Assessment Center, U.S. Secret Service, U.S. Department of Homeland Security, July 2019. As of March 31, 2021:
https://www.hsdl.org/?abstract&did=826876

Alathari, Lina, Diana Drysdale, Ashley Blair, Jeffrey McGarry, Catherine Camilletti, Amanda Snook, and Steven Driscoll, *Enhancing School Safety Using a Threat Assessment Model: An Operational Guide for Preventing Targeted School Violence*, Washington, D.C.: National Threat Assessment Center, U.S. Secret Service, U.S. Department of Homeland Security, July 2018. As of March 31, 2021:
https://www.cisa.gov/publication/
enhancing-school-safety-using-threat-assessment-model-operational-guide-preventing

Alathari, Lina, Diana Drysdale, Steven Driscoll, Ashley Blair, Arna Carlock, Aaron Cotkin, Brianna Johnston, Christina Foley, David Mauldin, Jeffrey McGarry, Jessica Nemet, Natalie Vineyard, and John Bullwinkel, *Protecting America's Schools: A U.S. Secret Service Analysis of Targeted School Violence*, Washington, D.C.: National Threat Assessment Center, U.S. Secret Service, U.S. Department of Homeland Security, 2019. As of March 31, 2021:
https://www.hsdl.org/?abstract&did=831141

Alathari, Lina, Diana Drysdale, Steven Driscoll, Ashley Blair, David Mauldin, Arna Carlock, Jeffrey McGarry, Aaron Cotkin, Jessica Nemet, Brianna Johnston, and Natalie Vineyard, *Mass Attacks in Public Spaces, 2019*, Washington, D.C.: National Threat Assessment Center, U.S. Secret Service, U.S. Department of Homeland Security, August 2020. As of March 31, 2021:
https://www.hsdl.org/?abstract&did=842250

Anti-Defamation League Center on Extremism, "ADL Hate Crime Map," undated a. As of May 22, 2021:
https://www.adl.org/adl-hate-crime-map

———, "ADL H.E.A.T. Map: Hate, Extremism, Antisemitism, Terrorism," undated b. As of May 22, 2021:
https://www.adl.org/education-and-resources/resource-knowledge-base/adl-heat-map

———, "ADL Tracker of Antisemitic Incidents," undated c. As of May 22, 2021:
https://www.adl.org/education-and-resources/resource-knowledge-base/adl-tracker-of-antisemitic-incidents
?field_incident_location_state_target_id=All&page=3

Aon, Continuum Economics, and Risk Advisory Group, "Aon Risk Maps," undated. As of May 24, 2021:
https://www.aon.com/2020-political-risk-terrorism-and-political-violence-maps/index.html

Armed Conflict Location and Event Data Project, "Data Export Tool," undated. As of May 22, 2021:
https://acleddata.com/data-export-tool/

BBC—*See* British Broadcasting Corporation.

Bergen, Peter, Albert Ford, Alyssa Sims, and David Sterman, *Terrorism in America After 9/11*, Washington,
D.C.: New America, International Security Program, 2020. As of February 9, 2021:
https://www.newamerica.org/in-depth/terrorism-in-america/

Bergen, Peter, David Sterman, and Melissa Salyk-Virk, "America's Counterterrorism Wars," New America, last
updated March 23, 2021. As of May 24, 2021:
https://www.newamerica.org/international-security/reports/americas-counterterrorism-wars/

Binder, Markus, "Profiles of Incidents Involving CBRN and Non-State Actors (POICN) Database," National
Consortium for the Study of Terrorism and Responses to Terrorism, undated. As of May 24, 2021:
https://www.start.umd.edu/research-projects/
profiles-incidents-involving-cbrn-and-non-state-actors-poicn-database

Bock, Lee, "An Experiment in Crowdscraping: A Look Back at Creating 'A Map of Terrorist Attacks,
According to Wikipedia," Esri, October 8, 2020. As of May 22, 2021:
https://storymaps.arcgis.com/stories/dcbb5c9e009442b99944bd1ef6158bda

Bowie, Neil Gordon, *The Application of Database Technologies to the Study of Terrorism and Counter-Terrorism:
A Post 9/11 Analysis*, Ph.D. thesis, University of St. Andrews, 2012. As of February 9, 2021:
https://research-repository.st-andrews.ac.uk/handle/10023/3641

———, "Terrorism Events Data: An Inventory of Databases and Data Sets, 1968–2017," *Perspectives on
Terrorism*, Vol. 11, No. 4, August 2017, pp. 50–72. As of February 9, 2021:
http://www.terrorismanalysts.com/pt/index.php/pot/article/view/622/html

———, "30 Terrorism Databases and Data Sets: A New Inventory," *Perspectives on Terrorism*, Vol. 12, No. 5,
October 2018, pp. 51–61. As of February 9, 2021:
https://www.universiteitleiden.nl/binaries/content/assets/customsites/perspectives-on-terrorism/2018/issue-5/
bowie.pdf

———, "A New Inventory of 30 Terrorism Databases and Data Sets," *Perspectives on Terrorism*, Vol. 14,
No. 1, February 2020, pp. 54–65. As of February 9, 2021:
https://www.jstor.org/stable/26891985?seq=1#metadata_info_tab_contents

Bowie, Neil G., and Alex P. Schmid, "Databases on Terrorism," in Alex P. Schmid, ed., *The Routledge
Handbook of Terrorism Research*, London: Routledge, 2011, pp. 294–340.

Brackstone, Gordon, "Managing Data Quality in a Statistical Agency," *Survey Methodology*, Vol. 25, No. 2,
December 1999, pp. 139–150.

British Broadcasting Corporation, "Who Are Britain's Jihadists?" October 12, 2017. As of May 22, 2021:
https://www.bbc.com/news/uk-32026985

Bruza, Emily, "Hate Crimes, Mass Casualty Attacks, and BIAS in America," *On the Homefront: The HSDL
Blog*, November 12, 2020. As of May 24, 2021:
https://www.hsdl.org/c/hate-crimes-mass-casualty/

B'Tselem, "Statistics," undated. As of May 22, 2021:
https://www.btselem.org/statistics

Bucci, Steven, James Carafano, and Jessica Zuckerman, "60 Terrorist Plots Since 9/11: Continued Lessons in Domestic Counterterrorism," Washington, D.C.: Heritage Foundation, July 22, 2013. As of May 24, 2021: https://www.heritage.org/terrorism/report/60-terrorist-plots-911-continued-lessons-domestic-counterterrorism

Bureau of Investigative Journalism, "Drone Warfare," undated. As of May 22, 2021: https://www.thebureauinvestigates.com/projects/drone-war

Canadian Network for Research on Terrorism, Security, and Society, "Canadian Incident Database (CIDB)," undated. As of May 22, 2021: https://www.tsas.ca/canadian-incident-database/

CBP—See U.S. Customs and Border Protection.

Center for Homeland Defense and Security, Naval Postgraduate School, "About the Project," undated a. As of April 1, 2021: https://www.chds.us/ssdb/about/

———, "Statistics," *Homeland Security Digital Library*, undated b. As of February 9, 2021: https://www.hsdl.org/?collection&id=2167

Center for International Security and Cooperation, Freeman Spogli Institute for International Studies, Stanford University, "Mapping Militants," undated. As of May 22, 2021: https://cisac.fsi.stanford.edu/mappingmilitants/mappingmilitants

Center for Strategic and International Studies, "Significant Cyber Incidents," undated. As of April 21, 2021: https://www.csis.org/programs/strategic-technologies-program/significant-cyber-incidents

Center for Terrorism and Intelligence Studies, "Research," undated. As of May 22, 2021: https://www.cetisresearch.org/research.htm

Center on Terrorism, Extremism, and Counterterrorism, Middlebury Institute of International Studies at Monterey, "Special Operations Research Database," undated. As of May 22, 2021: https://www.middlebury.edu/institute/academics/centers-initiatives/ctec/special-operations-research-database

Centers for Disease Control and Prevention, "Violence Prevention: School-Associated Violent Death Study," last reviewed October 24, 2019. As of May 22, 2021: https://www.cdc.gov/violenceprevention/youthviolence/schoolviolence/SAVD.html

———, "Injury Prevention and Control: Data and Statistics (WISQARS),"last reviewed July 1, 2020. As of May 22, 2021: https://www.cdc.gov/injury/wisqars/index.html

Centre for Terrorism and Counterterrorism, Leiden University, "Terrorism and Political Violence," undated. As of May 22, 2021: https://www.universiteitleiden.nl/en/research/research-projects/governance-and-global-affairs/terrorism-and-political-violence

Chapman, Sally, "National Counterterrorism Center's Worldwide Incidents Tracking System," Washington, D.C.: National Counterterrorism Center, May 9, 2006, updated April 1, 2016. As of May 24, 2021: https://www.hsdl.org/c/national-counterterrorism-centers-worldwide-incidents-tracking-system/

Chen, Hsinchun, "Dark Web Terrorism Research Community Resource Development (CRD)," Eller College of Management, University of Arizona, undated. As of May 24, 2021: https://eller.arizona.edu/departments-research/centers-labs/artificial-intelligence/research/previous/dark-web-geo-web/crd

Chicago Project on Security and Threats, University of Chicago, "The Database on Suicide Attacks (DSAT)," undated. As of May 22, 2021: https://cpost.uchicago.edu/research/suicide_attacks/database_on_suicide_attacks/

CISA—See Cybersecurity and Infrastructure Security Agency.

Clinical Data Interchange Standards Consortium, "CDISC Standards in the Clinical Research Process," undated. As of May 21, 2021: https://www.cdisc.org/standards

Combating Terrorism Center at West Point, U.S. Military Academy, "Harmony Program," undated. As of May 22, 2021:
https://ctc.usma.edu/harmony-program/

Conflict and Politics in Northern Ireland, Ulster University, homepage, last modified April 14, 2021. As of May 24, 2021:
https://cain.ulster.ac.uk/

Council on Foreign Relations, "Nigeria Security Tracker," last updated April 12, 2021a. As of May 22, 2021:
https://www.cfr.org/nigeria/nigeria-security-tracker/p29483

———, "Global Conflict Tracker," last updated May 21, 2021b. As of May 22, 2021:
https://www.cfr.org/global-conflict-tracker/

Counter Extremism Project, "Extremist Groups," undated a. As of May 22, 2021:
https://www.counterextremism.com/global_extremist_groups

———, "Terrorists and Extremists Database," undated b. As of May 22, 2021:
https://www.counterextremism.com/extremists

Countering Weapons of Mass Destruction Office, U.S. Department of Homeland Security, *Strategy, 2020–2040*, undated.

Cox, John Woodrow, Steven Rich, Allyson Chiu, John Muyskens, and Monica Ulmanu, "More Than 248,000 Students Have Experienced Gun Violence at School Since Columbine," *Washington Post*, updated March 31, 2021. As of April 1, 2021:
https://www.washingtonpost.com/graphics/2018/local/school-shootings-database/

Criminal Justice Information Services, Federal Bureau of Investigation, "Services," undated. As of May 22, 2021:
https://www.fbi.gov/services/cjis/ucr

CTC—*See* Combating Terrorism Center at West Point.

Cybersecurity and Infrastructure Security Agency, U.S. Department of Homeland Security, "CISA Strategic Intent—Defend Today, Secure Tomorrow," August 2019. As of February 9, 2021:
https://www.cisa.gov/publication/strategic-intent

DHS—*See* U.S. Department of Homeland Security.

Drysdale, Diana A., William Modzeleski, and Andre B. Simons, *Campus Attacks: Targeted Violence Affecting Institutions of Higher Education*, Washington, D.C.: U.S. Secret Service, U.S. Department of Education, and Federal Bureau of Investigation, April 2010. As of March 31, 2021:
https://www.hsdl.org/?abstract&did=26308

Duncan, Gillian, and Alex P. Schmid, "Bibliography of Terrorism," in Alex P. Schmid, ed., *The Routledge Handbook of Terrorism Research*, London: Routledge, 2011, pp. 475–597.

EBSCO Information Services, "International Security and Counter-Terrorism Reference Center," undated. As of May 22, 2021:
https://www.ebsco.com/products/research-databases/international-security-counter-terrorism-reference-center

Eck, Kristine, and Lisa Hultman, "Violence Against Civilians in War," *Journal of Peace Research*, Vol. 44, No. 2, 2007.

Enders, Walter, Todd Sandler, and Khusrav Gaibulloev, "Domestic Versus Transnational Terrorism: Data, Decomposition, and Dynamics," *Journal of Peace Research*, Vol. 48, No. 3, March 2011, pp. 319–337.

European Union Agency for Criminal Justice Cooperation, "Launch of Judicial Counter-Terrorism Register at Eurojust," press release, Brussels, September 5, 2019. As of May 22, 2021:
https://www.eurojust.europa.eu/launch-judicial-counter-terrorism-register-eurojust

Europol, "EU Terrorism Situation and Trend Report (TE-SAT)," undated. As of May 22, 2021:
https://www.europol.europa.eu/tesat-report

EveryStat, Everytown for Gun Safety, homepage, undated. As of May 22, 2021:
https://everystat.org/

Everytown Research and Policy, Everytown for Gun Safety, "Gunfire on School Grounds in the United States," undated. As of May 22, 2021:
https://everytownresearch.org/maps/gunfire-on-school-grounds/

FBI—*See* Federal Bureau of Investigation.

Federal Bureau of Investigation, "Don't Be A Puppet," undated.

Federal Emergency Management Agency, U.S. Department of Homeland Security, *2018–2022, Strategic Plan*, Washington, D.C., c. March 15, 2018. As of March 31, 2021:
https://www.hsdl.org/?abstract&did=808818

Federal Law Enforcement Training Centers, U.S. Department of Homeland Security, *Strategic Plan, 2018–2022*, Washington, D.C., undated. As of March 31, 2021:
https://www.fletc.gov/site-page/strategic-plan

FEMA—*See* Federal Emergency Management Agency.

Fjelde, Hanne, Lisa Hultman, Livia Schubiger, Lars-Erik Cederman, Simon Hug, and Margareta Sollenberg, "Introducing the Ethnic One-Sided Violence Dataset," *Conflict Management and Peace Science*, 2019.

Flight Safety Foundation, "ASN Aviation Safety Database," last updated May 22, 2021. As of May 22, 2021:
https://aviation-safety.net/database/

Follman, Mark, Gavin Aronsen, and Deanna Pan, "US Mass Shootings, 1982–2021: Data from Mother Jones' Investigation," *Mother Jones*, updated March 22, 2021. As of March 31, 2021:
https://www.motherjones.com/politics/2012/12/mass-shootings-mother-jones-full-data/

Forest, James J. F., *Terrorism and Counterterrorism: An Annotated Bibliography*, West Point, N.Y.: U.S. Military Academy, West Point, Department of Social Sciences, Combating Terrorism Center, March 22, 2004.

Forest, James J. F., Thomas A. Bengston, Jr., Hilda Rosa Martinez, Nathan Gonzalez, and Bridget C. Nee, *Terrorism and Counterterrorism: An Annotated Bibliography*, Vol. 2, West Point, N.Y.: U.S. Military Academy, West Point, Department of Social Sciences, Combating Terrorism Center, September 11, 2006. As of February 9, 2021:
https://www.hsdl.org/?abstract&did=785242

Freilich, Joshua D., Steven M. Chermak, Roberta Belli, Jeff Gruenewald, and William S. Parkin, "Introducing the United States Extremist Crime Database (ECDB)," *Terrorism and Political Violence*, Vol. 26, 2014, pp. 372–384.

George Washington University Program on Extremism, "Attacks: Jihadist Motivated Terrorist Attacks in Europe and North America," undated a. As of May 22, 2021:
https://extremism.gwu.edu/attacks

———, "ISIS in America: From Retweets to Raqqa," undated b. As of May 22, 2021:
https://extremism.gwu.edu/isis-america

———, "The Cases," undated c. As of May 22, 2021:
https://extremism.gwu.edu/cases

———, "GW Extremism Tracker: Terrorism in the U.S.," February 2021. As of February 9, 2021:
https://extremism.gwu.edu/gw-extremism-tracker

German Institute on Radicalization and De-Radicalization Studies, "Database on Terrorism in Germany: Right-Wing Extremism and Jihadism," last updated February 19, 2021. As of May 22, 2021:
http://girds.org/projects/database-on-terrorism-in-germany-right-wing-extremism

Gleditsch, Nils Petter, Peter Wallensteen, Mikael Eriksson, Margareta Sollenberg, and Håvard Strand, "Armed Conflict 1946–2001: A New Dataset," *Journal of Peace Research*, Vol. 39, No. 5, 2002.

Gordon, Avishag, "Terrorism and Knowledge Growth: A Databases and Internet Analysis," in Andrew Silke, ed., *Research on Terrorism: Trends, Achievements and Failures*, New York: Frank Cass, 2004, pp. 104–118.

Grossman, Andrew, "Update: A Research Guide to Cases and Materials on Terrorism," New York University, Hauser Global Law School Program, September–October 2017. As of February 9, 2021:
https://www.nyulawglobal.org/globalex/Terrorism1.html

Gun Violence Archive, "Mass Shootings in 2021," undated. As of May 22, 2021:
https://www.gunviolencearchive.org/reports/mass-shooting

GW Program on Extremism—*See* George Washington University Program on Extremism.

Hague Centre for Strategic Studies, "Jihadist Foreign Fighters Monitor (JihFFMON)," undated. As of
May 24, 2021:
https://dwh.hcss.nl/apps/ftf_monitor/

Homo, Kira, Christina H. Jones, and John Russell, *Terrorism: A Guide to Selected Resources*, Bloomington:
Indiana University, Center for the Study of Global Change, 2004.

Hull, Christopher C., "Lies, Damn Lies, and TEVUS: Evaluating the Terrorism and Extremist Violence in the
United States Database," Institute of World Politics, November 16, 2020. As of February 9, 2021:
https://www.iwp.edu/articles/2020/11/16/
lies-damn-lies-and-tevus-evaluating-the-terrorism-and-extremist-violence-in-the-united-states-database/

I&A—*See* Office of Intelligence and Analysis.

ICE—*See* U.S. Immigration and Customs Enforcement.

Institute for Conflict Management, South Asia Terrorism Portal, homepage, undated. As of May 24, 2021:
https://www.satp.org/

Institute for Security Studies, "Launch of Comprehensive African Counter-Terrorism Law and Policy
Database," press release, Pretoria, September 30, 2010. As of May 24, 2021:
https://issafrica.org/about-us/press-releases/
launch-of-comprehensive-african-counter-terrorism-law-and-policy-database

Institute for the Study of Violent Groups, homepage, undated.

Integrated Network for Societal Conflict Research, Center for Systemic Peace, "Data Page," undated. As of
May 24, 2021:
http://www.systemicpeace.org/inscrdata.html

IntelCenter, "IntelCenter Database (ICD)," undated a. As of May 24, 2021:
https://www.intelcenter.com/icd

———, "Terrorist Facial Recognition (TFR)," undated b. As of May 24, 2021:
https://www.intelcenter.com/tfr

International Atomic Energy Agency, "Incident and Trafficking Database (ITDB)," undated. As of May 24,
2021:
https://www.iaea.org/resources/databases/itdb

International Centre for Political Violence and Terrorism Research, S. Rajaratnam School of International
Studies, Nanyang Technological University, "Research Programmes," undated. As of May 24, 2021:
https://www.rsis.edu.sg/research/icpvtr/

International Crimes Database Project, homepage, undated. As of May 24, 2021:
http://www.internationalcrimesdatabase.org/Home

International Institute for Counter-Terrorism, Interdisciplinary Center Herzliya, "Database Desk," undated.
As of May 24, 2021:
https://www.ict.org.il/Articles.aspx?WordID=102#gsc.tab=0

International Institute for Strategic Studies, "The Armed Conflict Database," undated. As of May 24, 2021:
https://www.iiss.org/publications/armed-conflict-database

International Money Laundering Information Network, "AMLID," undated a. As of May 24, 2021:
https://www.imolin.org/imolin/amlid/index.jspx?lf_id=

———, "IMOLIN Case Law Database," undated b. As of May 24, 2021:
https://www.imolin.org/imolin/cld/search.jspx?lf_id=

International Terrorism: Attributes of Terrorist Events, homepage, undated. As of May 24, 2021:
https://library.duke.edu/data/sources/iterate

Investigative Project on Terrorism, "About the Investigative Project on Terrorism," undated a. As of April 1, 2021:
https://www.investigativeproject.org/about.php

———, "Court Cases," undated b. As of May 24, 2021:
https://www.investigativeproject.org/cases.php

———, "Groups and Individuals," undated c. As of May 24, 2021:
https://www.investigativeproject.org/profile/all/

IPT—*See* Investigative Project on Terrorism.

Jackson, Brian A., Ashley L. Rhoades, Jordan R. Reimer, Natasha Lander, Katherine Costello, and Sina Beaghley, *Practical Terrorism Prevention: Reexamining U.S. National Approaches to Addressing the Threat of Ideologically Motivated Violence*, Santa Monica, Calif.: RAND Corporation, RR-2647-DHS, 2019. As of February 9, 2021:
https://www.rand.org/pubs/research_reports/RR2647.html

Janes, "Terrorism and Insurgency," undated. As of May 24, 2021:
https://www.janes.com/military-threat-intelligence/terrorism-and-insurgency

Jewish Virtual Library, American–Israeli Cooperative Enterprise, "Terrorism Against Israel," undated. As of May 24, 2021:
https://www.jewishvirtuallibrary.org/terrorism-against-israel

John Jay and Artis Transnational Terrorism Database, "Welcome to the John Jay and Artis Transnational Terrorism Database," undated. As of May 24, 2021:
http://doitapps.jjay.cuny.edu/jjatt/index.php

Jongman, Berto, "Internet Websites and Links for (Counter-)Terrorism Research," *Perspectives on Terrorism*, Vol. 5, No. 1, March 2011, pp. 22–37. As of February 9, 2021:
http://www.terrorismanalysts.com/pt/index.php/pot/article/view/jongman-internet-websites/html

Kishi, Roudabeh, and Andrea Carboni, "Assessing Political Violence and Demonstrations in the United States: ACLED Pilot Data and Preliminary Findings," Armed Conflict Location and Event Data Project, November 5, 2019. As of May 22, 2021:
https://acleddata.com/2019/11/05/
assessing-political-violence-demonstrations-in-the-united-states-acled-pilot-data-preliminary-findings/

Kivu Security Tracker, homepage, undated. As of May 22, 2021:
https://kivusecurity.org/

LaFree, Gary, and Laura Dugan, "Introducing the Global Terrorism Database," *Terrorism and Political Violence*, May 2007, pp. 181–204. As of May 24, 2021:
https://www.start.umd.edu/publication/introducing-global-terrorism-database

LaFree, Gary, Brent Smith, Joshua Freilich, Steven Chermak, Erin Miller, William Braniff, and Kathleen Smarick, "The Terrorism and Extremist Violence in the United States (TEVUS) Database," National Consortium for the Study of Terrorism and Responses to Terrorism," undated. As of May 24, 2021:
https://www.start.umd.edu/research-projects/terrorism-and-extremist-violence-united-states-tevus-database

Laurine, Eric, "Empirical Databases of School Shootings," schoolshootingdatabase.com, undated. As of May 24, 2021:
https://www.schoolshootingdatabase.com/

Leadership Conference Education Fund, "Hate Magnified: Communities in Crisis," Communities Against Hate, undated. As of May 22, 2021:
https://hatemagnified.org/

Levitt, Matthew, "Lebanese Hezbollah Select Worldwide Activities Interactive Map and Timeline," Washington Institute for Near East Policy, August 1, 2020. As of May 24, 2021:
https://www.washingtoninstitute.org/policy-analysis/
lebanese-hezbollah-select-worldwide-activities-interactive-map-and-timeline

Malet, David, "The Foreign Fighter Project," undated. As of May 22, 2021:
https://davidmalet.com/foreign-fighter

Mattheis, A. A. M. B. Doty, A. Sin, M. Conley, C. Oh, S. Triana, and D. Antonetti, "UNC Dataset (Racially and Ethnically Motivated Violent Extremism and Targeted Violence Arrests 2011–2020)," London: Centre for Analysis of the Radical Right, August 13, 2020. As of May 22, 2021:
https://www.radicalrightanalysis.com/2020/08/13/
unc-dataset-racially-and-ethnically-motivated-violent-extremism-and-targeted-violence-arrests-2011-2020/

Maxwell, Lesli, Holly Peele, and Denisa R. Superville, "School Shootings This Year: How Many and Where—*Education Week*'s 2021 School Shooting Tracker," *Education Week*, March 1, 2021, updated May 6, 2021. As of May 22, 2021:
https://www.edweek.org/leadership/school-shootings-this-year-how-many-and-where/2021/03

Mayernik, Matthew S., "Open Data: Accountability and Transparency," *Big Data and Society*, Vol. 4, No. 2, July–December 2017, pp. 1–5. As of April 20, 2021:
https://doi.org/10.1177%2F2053951717718853

Meyer, Sam, Jakob Lengacher, and Jaewon Oh, "The CNS Global Incidents and Trafficking Database: What Do Seven Years of Incident Data Tell Us About Global Nuclear Security?" Washington, D.C.: Nuclear Threat Initiative, December 8, 2020. As of May 24, 2021:
https://www.nti.org/analysis/articles/cns-global-incidents-and-trafficking-database/

Miller, Erin, Gary LaFree, and Laura Dugan, "Global Terrorism Database (GTD)," undated. As of February 9, 2021:
https://www.start.umd.edu/data-tools/global-terrorism-database-gtd

Miller, Erin, and Kathleen Smarick, "Profiles of Perpetrators of Terrorism in the United States," National Consortium for the Study of Terrorism and Responses to Terrorism, undated. As of May 24, 2021:
https://www.start.umd.edu/data-tools/profiles-perpetrators-terrorism-united-states-ppt-us

Mineta Transportation Institute, "Protecting Transit and Passenger Rail from Terrorism," press release, *Mass Transit*, March 3, 2017. As of May 24, 2021:
https://www.masstransitmag.com/safety-security/press-release/12311734/
mineta-transportation-institute-mti-protecting-transit-and-passenger-rail-from-terrorism

Minorities at Risk Project, homepage, last updated June 8, 2016. As of May 24, 2021:
http://www.mar.umd.edu/

Monterey Terrorism Research and Education Program, "Monterey WMD Terrorism Database," undated. As of May 24, 2021:
http://wmddb.miis.edu/

Muslim Public Affairs Council, "Post-9/11 Terrorism Database," April 23, 2013. As of May 24, 2021:
https://www.mpac.org/publications/policy-papers/post-911-terrorism-database.php

National Consortium for the Study of Terrorism and Responses to Terrorism, "About the GTD," undated a. As of April 1, 2021:
https://start.umd.edu/gtd/about/

———, "Global Terrorism Database," undated b. As of May 24, 2021:
https://www.start.umd.edu/gtd/

———, "Terrorism and Preparedness Data Resource Center (TPDRC)," undated c. As of May 24, 2021:
https://www.start.umd.edu/data-tools/terrorism-preparedness-data-resource-center-tpdrc

National Institute of Corrections, U.S. Department of Justice, "National Archive of Criminal Justice Data (NACJD)," undated. As of May 21, 2021:
https://nicic.gov/national-archive-criminal-justice-data-nacjd

National Police Foundation, "Averted School Violence Data Collection Platform," undated. As of May 24, 2021:
https://www.policefoundation.org/averted-school-attacks-data-collection-platform/

National School Safety and Security Services, "School Associated Violent Deaths and School Shootings," undated. As of May 24, 2021:
https://www.schoolsecurity.org/trends/violent-deaths-and-school-shootings/

National Threat Assessment Center, U.S. Secret Service, U.S. Department of Homeland Security, *Attacks on Federal Government, 2001–2013: Threat Assessment Considerations*, Washington, D.C., December 2015. As of March 31, 2021:
https://www.hsdl.org/?abstract&did=788758

Naval Postgraduate School, Dudley Knox Library, "Terrorism Databases," updated March 19, 2021. As of February 9, 2021:
https://libguides.nps.edu/terror/special

NTAC—*See* National Threat Assessment Center.

O'Brien, Beth, "Muslim-American Involvement with Violent Extremism, 2001–2020," Triangle Center on Terrorism and Homeland Security, Sanford School of Public Policy, Duke University, January 14, 2021. As of May 24, 2021:
https://sites.duke.edu/tcths/2021/01/14/muslim-american-involvement-with-violent-extremism-2001-2020/

Odhikar, "Statistics on Political Violence," undated. As of May 24, 2021:
http://odhikar.org/statistics/statistics-on-political-violence/

Office of the Assistant Secretary for Planning and Evaluation, U.S. Department of Health and Human Services, "U.S. Department of Health and Human Services Implementation Guidance on Data Collection Standards for Race, Ethnicity, Sex, Primary Language, and Disability Status," October 2011. As of March 24, 2021:
https://aspe.hhs.gov/basic-report/hhs-implementation-guidance-data-collection-standards-race-ethnicity-sex-primary-language-and-disability-status

Office of Intelligence and Analysis, U.S. Department of Homeland Security, *Strategic Plan, FY 2020–2024*, Washington, D.C., February 6, 2020. As of March 31, 2021:
https://www.dhs.gov/publication/office-intelligence-and-analysis-fy-2020-2024-strategic-plan

Pak Institute for Peace Studies, homepage, undated. As of May 24, 2021:
https://www.pakpips.com/

Pakistan Institute for Conflict and Security Studies, "PICSS Database of Anti-State Violence," undated. As of May 24, 2021:
https://www.picss.net/picss-database-of-anti-state-violence-in-pakistan/

Perliger, Arie, *Counterterrorism Reading List*, West Point, N.Y.: Combating Terrorism Center at West Point, October 2010. As of March 19, 2021:
https://www.ctc.usma.edu/counterterrorism-reading-list/

Pettersson, Therese, and Magnus Öberg, "Organized Violence, 1989–2019," *Journal of Peace Research*, Vol. 57, No. 4, 2020.

PIPS—*See* Pak Institute for Peace Studies.

Political Terror Scale, "Documentation: Coding Rules," undated. As of April 1, 2021:
http://www.politicalterrorscale.org/Data/Documentation.html

Pollack, William S., William Modzeleski, and Georgann Rooney, *Prior Knowledge of Potential School-Based Violence: Information Students Learn May Prevent a Targeted Attack*, Washington, D.C., U.S. Secret Service and U.S. Department of Education, May 2008. As of March 31, 2021:
https://www.hsdl.org/?abstract&did=486114

Project on Violent Conflict, Rockefeller College of Public Affairs and Policy, University at Albany, State University of New York, "Current Projects," undated. As of May 24, 2021:
https://www.albany.edu/pvc/current_projects.shtml

PTS—*See* Political Terror Scale.

Public Law 107-296, Homeland Security Act of 2002, November 25, 2002. As of May 12, 2019:
https://www.govinfo.gov/app/details/PLAW-107publ296

Public Law 114-267, Northern Border Security Review Act, December 14, 2016. As of March 22, 2021:
https://www.govinfo.gov/app/details/PLAW-114publ267

Public Law 114-328, National Defense Authorization Act for Fiscal Year 2017, December 23, 2016. As of March 22, 2021:
https://www.govinfo.gov/app/details/PLAW-114publ328

Public Law 115-91, National Defense Authorization Act for Fiscal Year 2018, December 12, 2017. As of March 22, 2021:
https://www.govinfo.gov/app/details/PLAW-115publ91

Public Law 115-331, Department of Homeland Security Data Framework Act of 2018, December 19, 2018. As of March 22, 2021:
https://www.govinfo.gov/app/details/PLAW-115publ331

Public Law 115-400, Vehicular Terrorism Prevention Act of 2018, December 31, 2018. As of February 9, 2021:
https://www.govinfo.gov/app/details/PLAW-115publ400

Public Law 116-92, National Defense Authorization Act for Fiscal Year 2020, December 20, 2019. As of March 22, 2021:
https://www.govinfo.gov/app/details/PLAW-116publ92

Public Law 116-116, DHS Field Engagement Accountability Act, March 2, 2020. As of March 22, 2021:
https://www.govinfo.gov/app/details/PLAW-116publ116

Qureshi, Aisha Javed, "Understanding Domestic Radicalization and Terrorism: A National Issue Within a Global Context," Washington, D.C.: National Institute of Justice, August 14, 2020. As of February 9, 2021:
https://nij.ojp.gov/topics/articles/understanding-domestic-radicalization-and-terrorism

RAND Corporation, "RAND Database of Worldwide Terrorism Incidents," Santa Monica, Calif., undated. As of February 9, 2021:
https://www.rand.org/nsrd/projects/terrorism-incidents.html

Ravndal, Jacob Aasland, "Right-Wing Terrorism and Violence in Western Europe: Introducing the RTV Dataset," *Perspectives on Terrorism*, Vol. 10, No. 3, June 2016. As of May 22, 2021:
http://www.terrorismanalysts.com/pt/index.php/pot/article/view/508

Ritchie, Hannah, Joe Hasell, Cameron Appel, and Max Roser, "Terrorism," Our World in Data, July 2013, last revised November 2019. As of May 24, 2021:
https://ourworldindata.org/terrorism

Rosendorff, B. Peter, and Todd Sandler, "The Political Economy of Transnational Terrorism," *Journal of Conflict Resolution*, Vol. 49, No. 2, April 2005, pp. 171–182.

Salehyan, Idean, Cullen S. Hendrix, Jesse Hamner, Christina Case, Christopher Linebarger, Emily Stull, and Jennifer Williams, "Social Conflict in Africa: A New Database," *International Interactions*, Vol. 38, No. 4, 2012, pp. 503–511. As of May 24, 2021:
https://www.strausscenter.org/ccaps-research-areas/social-conflict/database/

Schmid, Alex Peter, and Albert J. Jongman, *Political Terrorism: A New Guide to Actors, Authors, Concepts, Data Bases, Theories, and Literature*, New Brunswick, N.J.: Transaction Books, 1988.

Sheehan, Ivan Sascha, "Assessing and Comparing Data Sources for Terrorism Research," in Cynthia Lum and Leslie W. Kennedy, eds., *Evidence-Based Counterterrorism Policy*, New York: Springer, 2011, pp. 13–40.

Smith, Brent L., "Sequencing Terrorists' Precursor Behaviors: A Crime Specific Analysis, United States, 1980–2012," Inter-university Consortium for Political and Social Research [distributor], April 23, 2018. As of May 24, 2021:
https://www.icpsr.umich.edu/web/NACJD/studies/36676

———, "Longevity of American Terrorists: Factors Affecting Sustainability, [United States], 1980–2015 (ICPSR 37175)," Inter-university Consortium for Political and Social Research [distributor], August 29, 2019. As of May 24, 2021:
https://www.icpsr.umich.edu/web/NACJD/studies/37175

Smith, Brent L., David A. Snow, Kevin Fitzpatrick, Kelly R. Damphousse, Paxton Roberts, Anna Tan, Andy Brooks, and Brent Klein, "Identity and Framing Theory, Precursor Activity, and the Radicalization Process," National Consortium for the Study of Terrorism and Responses to Terrorism, undated. As of May 24, 2021:
https://www.start.umd.edu/publication/
identity-and-framing-theory-precursor-activity-and-radicalization-process

Southern Poverty Law Center, "Extremist Files," undated. As of May 24, 2021:
https://www.splcenter.org/fighting-hate/extremist-files

———, "Hate in the United States," February 16, 2021. As of May 24, 2021:
https://www.splcenter.org/hate-map

Stanford Mass Shootings of America, "Mass Shootings in America," undated. As of May 24, 2021:
https://library.stanford.edu/projects/mass-shootings-america

START—*See* National Consortium for the Study of Terrorism and Responses to Terrorism.

Stockholm International Peace Research Institute, "Arms Embargoes," undated. As of May 24, 2021:
https://www.sipri.org/databases/embargoes

———, "Global Registry of Violent Deaths Website Launches, SIPRI Convenor," press release, March 25, 2020. As of May 24, 2021:
https://www.sipri.org/news/2020/global-registry-violent-deaths-website-launches-sipri-convenor

Strong, Diane M., Yang W. Lee, and Richard Y. Wang, "Data Quality in Context," *Communications of the ACM*, Vol. 40, No. 5, May 1997, pp. 103–110.

Sundberg, Ralph, Kristine Eck, and Joakim Kreutz, "Introducing the UCDP Non-State Conflict Dataset," *Journal of Peace Research*, Vol. 49, No. 2, 2012.

Sundberg, Ralph, and Erik Melander, "Introducing the UCDP Georeferenced Event Dataset," *Journal of Peace Research*, Vol. 50, No. 4, 2013.

Terrorism and Extremist Violence in the United States Analyst Portal, "TEVUS," undated. As of April 1, 2021:
https://tap.cast.uark.edu/

Terrorism Research and Analysis Consortium, homepage, undated.

Terrorism Research Center, University of Arkansas, homepage, undated. As of May 24, 2021:
https://terrorismresearch.uark.edu/

Terrorism Research Initiative, "Recommended Data Sources for the Study of Terrorism," *Teaching About Terrorism: A Resource Portal of the Terrorism Research Initiative*, undated. As of February 9, 2021:
http://www.teachingterror.com/data.htm

TEVUS Analyst Portal—*See* Terrorism and Extremist Violence in the United States Analyst Portal.

Tinnes, Judith, "100 Core and Periphery Journals for Terrorism Research," *Perspectives on Terrorism*, Vol. 7, No. 2, April 2013, pp. 96–103. As of February 9, 2021:
http://www.terrorismanalysts.com/pt/index.php/pot/article/view/258

———, "Bibliography: Terrorism Research Literature (Part 1)," *Perspectives on Terrorism*, Vol. 8, No. 1, February 2014, pp. 99–132. As of February 9, 2021:
http://www.terrorismanalysts.com/pt/index.php/pot/article/view/328/659

Transportation Security Administration, U.S. Department of Homeland Security, *TSA Strategy 2018–2026*, undated. As of February 9, 2021:
https://www.tsa.gov/about/strategy

———, *2020 Biennial National Strategy for Transportation Security*, report to Congress, May 29, 2020a. As of February 9, 2021:
https://www.dhs.gov/publication/2020-biennial-national-strategy-transportation-security

———, *Administrator's Intent 2.0*, June 2020b. As of February 9, 2021:
https://www.hsdl.org/?abstract&did=840207

TSA—*See* Transportation Security Administration.

UCDP—*See* Uppsala Conflict Data Program.

UCR—*See* Uniform Crime Reporting.

UK Home Office—*See* United Kingdom Home Office.

"UMass Professor Analyzes Far-Right Violence," *The [Lowell] Sun*, September 14, 2020. As of May 24, 2021:
https://www.lowellsun.com/2020/09/14/umass-professor-analyzes-far-right-violence/

Uniform Crime Reporting, Federal Bureau of Investigation, U.S. Department of Justice, "Hate Crime Statistics," undated. As of April 1, 2021:
https://www.fbi.gov/services/cjis/ucr/hate-crime

United Kingdom Home Office, "Counter Terrorism Statistics," last updated March 4, 2017. As of May 24, 2021:
https://www.gov.uk/government/collections/counter-terrorism-statistics

Uppsala Conflict Data Program, Department of Peace and Conflict Research, Uppsala University, "UCDP Dataset Download Center," undated. As of April 1, 2021:
https://ucdp.uu.se/downloads/

"US Airstrikes in the Long War," *Long War Journal*, undated. As of May 24, 2021:
https://www.longwarjournal.org/us-airstrikes-in-the-long-war

U.S. Citizenship and Immigration Services, U.S. Department of Homeland Security, *2019–2021 Strategic Plan*, Washington, D.C., undated. As of March 31, 2021:
https://www.hsdl.org/?abstract&did=823434

U.S. Coast Guard, *Coast Guard Strategic Plan, 2018–2022*, Washington, D.C., undated. As of February 9, 2021:
https://www.uscg.mil/Portals/0/seniorleadership/alwaysready/
USCG_Strategic%20Plan__LoResReaderSpreads_20181115_vFinal.pdf?ver=2018-11-14-150015-323

U.S. Code, Title 6, Domestic Security; Chapter 1, Homeland Security Organization; Subchapter III, Science and Technology in Support of Homeland Security; Section 185, Federally Funded Research and Development Centers. As of March 20, 2021:
https://uscode.house.gov/view.xhtml?req=(title:6%20section:185%20edition:prelim)

U.S. Customs and Border Protection, U.S. Department of Homeland Security, "Strategy 2020–2025: Mission, Team, Future," April 2019. As of February 9, 2021:
https://www.cbp.gov/document/publications/u-s-customs-and-border-protection-strategy-2020-2025

U.S. Department of Homeland Security, *Quadrennial Homeland Security Review*, 2014. As of February 9, 2021:
https://www.dhs.gov/publication/2014-quadrennial-homeland-security-review-qhsr

———, *Northern Border Strategy*, June 2018. As of February 9, 2021:
https://www.dhs.gov/publication/northern-border-strategy#

———, "Guiding Principles," July 3, 2019a. As of February 9, 2021:
https://www.dhs.gov/guiding-principles

———, *The DHS Strategic Plan: Fiscal Years 2020–2024*, July 3, 2019b. As of February 9, 2021:
https://www.dhs.gov/publication/department-homeland-securitys-strategic-plan-fiscal-years-2020-2024

———, *Strategic Framework for Countering Terrorism and Targeted Violence*, September 2019c. As of February 9, 2021:
https://www.dhs.gov/publication/strategic-framework-countering-terrorism-and-targeted-violence

———, "Strategic Framework for Countering Terrorism and Targeted Violence: Public Action Plan," September 2020a. As of February 9, 2021:
https://www.dhs.gov/news/2020/09/11/
dhs-public-action-plan-implement-strategic-framework-countering-terrorism-and

———, *Homeland Threat Assessment*, October 2020b. As of February 9, 2021:
https://www.dhs.gov/publication/2020-homeland-threat-assessment

———, *2020 National Preparedness Report*, December 22, 2020c. As of March 23, 2021:
https://www.fema.gov/emergency-managers/national-preparedness#reports

U.S. Immigration and Customs Enforcement, U.S. Department of Homeland Security, *Strategic Plan, 2021–2025*, Washington, D.C., August 2020. As of February 9, 2021:
https://www.ice.gov/doclib/about/pdf/iceStratPlan2021-2025.pdf

U.S. Secret Service, U.S. Department of Homeland Security, *United States Secret Service FY 2018–FY 2022 Strategic Plan*, Washington, D.C., May 2018. As of March 31, 2021:
https://www.hsdl.org/?abstract&did=822510

Verisk Maplecroft, "Terrorism Index," undated. As of May 24, 2021:
https://www.maplecroft.com/risk-indices/terrorism-index/

Vidino, Lorenzo, Jon Lewis, and Andrew Mines, "Dollars for Daesh: The Small Financial Footprint of the Islamic State's American Supporters," *CTC Sentinel*, Vol. 13, No. 3, March 2020. As of May 22, 2021:
https://ctc.usma.edu/dollars-daesh-small-financial-footprint-islamic-states-american-supporters/

Vinyard Software, "International Terrorism Data Center," undated. As of May 24, 2021:
https://vinyardsoftware.com/

Violence Project, "Mass Shooter Database," undated. As of May 24, 2021:
https://www.theviolenceproject.org/mass-shooter-database/

von Uexkull, Nina, and Therese Pettersson, "Codebook UCDP Non-State Conflict Issues and Actors Dataset," version 1.0, Department of Peace and Conflict Research, Uppsala University, 2018. As of April 1, 2021:
https://ucdp.uu.se/downloads/nonstateconflict/Codebook_nsissues.pdf

Vossekuil, Bryan, Robert A. Fein, Marisa Reddy, Randy Borum, and William Modzeleski, *The Final Report and Findings of the Safe School Initiative: Implications for the Prevention of School Attacks in the United States*, Washington, D.C., U.S. Secret Service and U.S. Department of Education, May 2002. As of March 31, 2021:
https://www.schoolsafety.gov/resource/
final-report-and-findings-safe-school-initiative-implications-prevention-school-attacks-0

Wang, Kevin, Phil Kott, and Andrew Moore, *Assessing the Relationship Between Interviewer Effects and NSDUH Data Quality*, Raleigh, N.C.: RTI International, prepared for the Substance Abuse and Mental Health Services Administration, October 24, 2013. As of March 31, 2021:
https://www.samhsa.gov/data/report/
assessing-relationship-between-interviewer-effects-and-nsduh-data-quality

Wang, Richard Y., and Diane M. Strong, "Beyond Accuracy: What Data Quality Means to Data Consumers," *Journal of Management Information Systems*, Vol. 12, No. 4, 1996, pp. 5–33.

Wilkenfeld, Jonathan, and R. Karl Rethemeyer, "Terrorist and Extremist Organizations (TEO) Database," National Consortium for the Study of Terrorism and Responses to Terrorism, undated. As of May 24, 2021:
https://www.start.umd.edu/research-projects/terrorist-and-extremist-organizations-teo-database

Willis, Henry H., Mary Tighe, Andrew Lauland, Liisa Ecola, Shoshana R. Shelton, Meagan L. Smith, John G. Rivers, Kristin J. Leuschner, Terry Marsh, and Daniel M. Gerstein, *Homeland Security National Risk Characterization: Risk Assessment Methodology*, Santa Monica, Calif.: RAND Corporation, RR-2140-DHS, 2018. As of March 23, 2021:
https://www.rand.org/pubs/research_reports/RR2140.html

Yates, Elizabeth, Gary LaFree, Michael Jensen, Sheehan Kane, Mehmet Adil Yalcin, Anita Atwell Seate, and Daniela Pisoiu, "Profiles of Individual Radicalization in the United States (PIRUS)," National Consortium for the Study of Terrorism and Responses to Terrorism, undated. As of May 24, 2021:
https://www.start.umd.edu/data-tools/profiles-individual-radicalization-united-states-pirus